Wildest Dreams

A play

Alan Ayckbourn

Samuel French — London
New York - Toronto - Hollywood

Please see page iv for further copyright information

Printed at Redwood Books, Trowbridge, Wiltshire.

WILDEST DREAMS

First performed at the Stephen Joseph Theatre in the Round, Scarborough, on 6th May 1991, with the following cast:

Stanley Inchbridge	Barry McCarthy
Hazel Inchbridge	Anna Keaveney
Warren Wrigley	Gary Whitaker
Rick Toller	Isabel Lloyd
Marcie Banks	Rebecca Lacey
Austen Skate	Peter Laird
Thelma Wrigley	Elizabeth Rider
Larry Banks	Glyn Grain

Director Alan Ayckbourn
Designer Roger Glossop
Lighting Mick Hughes

Subsequently performed by the Royal Shakespeare Company in The Pit on 14th December 1993, with the following cast:

Stanley Inchbridge	Barry McCarthy
Hazel Inchbridge	Brenda Blethyn
Warren Wrigley	Gary Whitaker
Rick Toller	Jenna Russell
Marcie Banks	Sophie Thompson
Austen Skate	Peter Laird
Thelma Wrigley	Andree Evans
Larry Banks	Paul Bentall

Director Alan Ayckbourn
Designer Roger Glossop
Lighting Mick Hughes

COPYRIGHT INFORMATION

(See also page ii)

CHARACTERS

Stanley Inchbridge (Alric, the Old Wise One); 48
Hazel Inchbridge (Idonia, The Child of Many
  Tongues); 43
Warren Wrigley (Xenon, The Stranger); 17
Rick Toller (Herwin, The Battle Companion); 21
Marcie Banks (Novia, The Newcomer); 22
Austen Skate; 50
Thelma Wrigley; 40
Larry Banks; 35
Pat Toller (voice only)
Ken Martin (voice only)

The action of the play takes place in the Inchbridges'
sitting-room, Warren's attic and Rick's basement

Time — one December

Other plays by Alan Ayckbourn published by
Samuel French Ltd:

Absent Friends
Absurd Person Singular
Bedroom Farce
A Chorus of Disapproval
Confusions
A Cut in the Rates
Ernie's Incredible Illucinations
Henceforward ...
How the Other Half Loves
Intimate Exchanges Volume 1
Intimate Exchanges Volume 2
Joking Apart
Just Between Ourselves
Living Together
Man of the Moment
Mixed Doubles (with other authors)
Mr A's Amazing Maze Plays
Mr Whatnot
The Norman Conquests
Relatively Speaking
The Revengers' Comedies
Round and Round the Garden
Season's Greetings
A Small Family Business
Suburban Strains
Table Manners
Taking Steps
Ten Times Table
Time and Time Again
Time of My Life
Tons of Money (revised)
Way Upstream
Wolf at the Door
Woman in Mind

ACT I

Scene 1

Three rooms

The main area is taken up with Hazel and Stanley Inchbridge's ground-floor sitting-room. Or, more correctly, the sitting-room which Hazel and Stanley occasionally occupy, since, as he never ceases to remind them, a good half of the room is the property of Hazel's brother, Austen Skate. It is an unexceptional front room in an ordinary, modern semi-detached house in an unremarkable street in an undistinguished town. The furnishings consist of a two- or three-piece suite, one or two occasional tables and four upright chairs (a couple of them apparently gathered from other parts of the house), grouped round a drop-leaf table which is presently extended and pulled out into the centre of the room. A "coal-effect" electric or gas fire. A bright overhead "chandelier" and one or two table or standard lamps. A sideboard with a foolscap envelope on it. One door and a bow window

A slightly smaller area represents the basement in Rick (Alice) Toller's house. This, by contrast, is dirty and untidy — a tip. It was possibly the old kitchen or scullery of the large Victorian terraced house of which it is part. It doesn't look as if it's been properly redecorated since. There is a little light from either the barred subterranean windows or the inadequate overhead naked bulb. A camp bed in the corner. A small table. An easy chair. An upright chair. A small electric fire. Other junk. There are three exits, one via a door, presumably once the tradesman's entrance, leading directly to the outside and the basement-area steps, another, via a flight of stairs, up to the ground floor of the house. The third exit is a doorway that apparently links through to the rest of the cellar

The third playing area is even smaller. This is the attic in a modern estate house. It has been converted into Warren Wrigley's study-bedroom-den. It consists almost entirely of computers or computer-driven equipment. There is a swivel chair in the midst of it from which Warren controls his world. A small bed in the corner. Orderly piles of computer magazines and books. Warren is a creature of method and tidiness. There is only one entrance to this room, which is via a trap door in the floor. This leads to the first-floor landing of the house, though we see nothing of this, just the tip of an extending metal ladder which provides access

As the Curtain *rises only the Inchbridges' sitting-room is lit, and that very sparingly, even dramatically, by a clip-on anglepoise lamp fastened to the edge of the main table. The light is thus cast downwards on to the surface, which is entirely covered by the map of the Game. This consists of a simple light-coloured board subdivided into squares. These are permanently etched on and sealed in, allowing players to draw in crayon over the board to mark out temporary features which can later be erased. Several of these are drawn at present, marking rivers and topographical features in different colours*

There are four model figures occupying four adjacent squares, apparently in the process of crossing the board. Like the board, these are good even if they are home-made. The first of them is the figure of a wise "ancient", Alric, stooped and elderly, with a stick and flowing robes. The second, Idonia, the mystic and magical one, childlike, beautiful in a dress and with a mane of flowing hair. Next, a strange green-faced creature, half man, half beast — Xenon — the stranger or alien, possessor of special powers of sight and hearing. Finally, the compact, powerful figure of Herwin, the masculine-named female warrior, armoured, carrying a broadsword drawn, shield held ready in case of sudden attack

The light from the board is reflected upwards into the faces of four people controlling these figures. Moving Alric is Stanley Inchbridge, in his forties, of slight build, a schoolteacher with a gentle but sadly often ineffectual disposition. Controlling Idonia is his wife, Hazel. Never a great beauty, time has not treated Hazel kindly. A few years younger than Stanley, she looks every bit her age despite, or perhaps indeed because of, her frenzied attempts to keep middle age at bay. Warren Wrigley controls the half-man, half-beast Xenon. Warren is about seventeen, a pupil of Stanley. A large boy with more than his fair share of spots, he is a boffin and a loner. Warren has no friends of his own age, nor does he any longer seek them, preferring the company of adults such as Stanley and Hazel, with whom he is at ease and outgoing; this couple have become almost surrogate parents to him. All Warren lacks is a girl. But they too avoid him. Especially the fourth member of the group, Rick (Alice) Toller, who is represented on the board by Herwin, the warrior. Rick is in her early twenties, small and undernourished. She appears to have a permanent cold. She makes little of her appearance and doesn't care. She rarely speaks. She's the introvert of the group. Troubled and private. Yet somehow, thanks to Stanley and Hazel's coaxing and encouragement, she finds her way to their house once a week

At present, the group are all gazing intently at the playing board — their concentration absolute. The "voices" their characters use are not overdone

Hazel (*in a child's voice*) Whither shall we proceed, Alric, O Wise Leader?

Stanley (*an older voice*) We must ask that of Xenon, the Far-sighted One. Whither now, Xenon?

Warren (*a slight singsong "alien" tone*) I look, Ancient One. With my great non-human sight, I look. To the north are hills, the Mountains of Ag. Beyond that lies the Kingdom of Endocia, the Virgin Queen, Ruler of the Fish People. To the west, the Kingdom of Orrich, Lord of all Oak Trees and the Forest of Emptiness. To the east, the Grey River, which winds into the Valley of Disappointment and Despair.

Stanley And to the south?

Warren There lie-eth the Dead Place. The land ruled over by Balaac, the Beast.

Hazel (*breathlessly*) Balaac!

Warren With my great hearing I hear him. I hear his footfalls.

Hazel Then that's the way we must go!

Stanley Ah, yes. but caution, caution. Despite your gifts, you are still a child and impetuous, Idonia. We must prepare and gather our strength. Only then may we hope to attack and win against Balaac, the Beast.

Warren True. True. The Old One speaks true.

Stanley We must prepare ourselves. Are we all agreed?

Hazel We are agreed, O Venerable and Wise Leader.

Warren You speak wisely, Ancient One.

Stanley What say you, Herwin, Silent Battle Warrior?

Hazel Herwin? What say you?

Rick (*muttering, self-consciously*) Yes, fine. That's OK by me.

Hazel (*prompting, a little impatiently*) O Wise Leader.

Rick O Wise Leader.

Stanley When next we meet, then, it is to the south we travel. What dangers foresee you for us, Idonia, Enchantress and Child of Many Tongues?

Hazel (*using one of her many tongues*) Daire-straidle more-dardle-haire. Alric, Wise One, I see-eth much danger for us all. Even Herwin, the Warrior, needeth all her strength to defeat the might of the Evil Balaac. Yea, even Xenon, the Stranger, needeth all his mighty unworldly powers. Broole-hardle.

Warren Xenon will be ready. And so will Herwin, the Fearless. (*To Rick*) Won't you?

Rick Yeah.

Stanley So be it. It is agreed. Then onward!

Hazel Onward!

Rick Onward!

Stanley But now let us pitch camp, for I, the oldest amongst you, would fain rest before our journey.

4 Wildest Dreams

Hazel We will rest with you, O Leader.
Stanley (*less authoritatively*) And also it is now (*glancing at his watch*) just
after twenty to ten, so I think it's probably time to break it up for this
evening.
Hazel (*rising*) Heavens! Is that the time? (*She switches on the overhead light.
The room is suddenly very bright*)
Stanley Yes, I'm afraid that little adventure will have to wait until next
Thursday.
Hazel I didn't realize it was that late. He'll be back in a minute demanding
his sandwiches.

*Stanley unplugs and unfastens the anglepoise. Warren puts away the game
pieces and folds up the board*

Rick goes into the hall

Stanley Ah, well, once you're in that other world ...
Hazel (*drily*) ... some of us don't want to leave it ...
Stanley Well, I wouldn't say that, I wouldn't say that, Hazel. It's only a bit
of fun, you know. That's all.

*Hazel goes out, taking one of the chairs which belongs in the kitchen, as
she says the following*

Hazel Oh dear, we mustn't get fun muddled up with life, must we? Fatal.
Stanley (*ignoring this*) Thank you very much, Warren. The usual place,
would you?
Warren Yes, Mr Inchbridge. (*He puts the board and figures, in a box, away
in a sideboard drawer*)
Stanley And I think again we have to thank you for another exciting
adventure tonight, Warren. Well done.
Warren Thank you, Mr Inchbridge.

*Rick returns, during the next, from the hall, fastening up her motor-cycling
gear*

Stanley That snake monster was quite vivid. Terrifying.
Warren Worm. It was a worm.
Stanley Worm. Sorry, yes.
Warren Tagarth of the Worm People.
Stanley Ah, well, we made short work of that. Thanks to Herwin there.

Rick manages a brief smile

Hazel returns for the second kitchen chair

Warren heads towards the hall to put his coat on

You're off, then, Rick, are you?
Rick Yes. I've got to get back.
Hazel You've got enough to eat at home now, have you? (*She hands Warren the chair*) Take this with you, Warren.

Warren exits with the chair

(*To Rick*) Have you got food in?
Rick Yes.
Hazel You eating properly?
Rick Yes, when I want to.
Hazel Whatever that means. We've got half a pie left in the fridge. A steak and kidney pie. I'll wrap that up for you.
Rick No, really ...
Stanley She's all right, Hazel.
Hazel None of us are going to eat it, are we? You're not. You just sit there picking out the kidney. And Austen refuses to eat reheated meat. It'll only go to waste.
Rick I'm fine, really. No problem. Night.

Rick moves to exit

Warren enters at this point wearing his anorak and scarf. He allows Rick to pass him in the doorway

Warren (*to Rick*) Night.
Stanley Good-night, Rick.

Rick escapes and goes

You mustn't crowd that girl, you know, Hazel.
Hazel It's stupid. I'll only finish up throwing it away.
Stanley She can't balance a great pie dish on her motorbike, can she? Are you off, Warren?
Hazel (*gathering up the lamp from the table*) I could have wrapped it up for her.
Warren Yes, Mr Inchbridge. Thank you.

Hazel goes out with the anglepoise lamp, speaking as she goes

Hazel I'd've put a bag round it for her. Now it's just going to go to waste, isn't it ... ?

Stanley picks up the foolscap envelope from the sideboard

Stanley Thank you for this, Warren. I'll certainly have a look at it before next week. It's a short story, you say?

Warren It's in the form of a personal statement, Mr Inchbridge. Based on scientifically proved facts.

Stanley (*politely*) Oh, how interesting.

Warren It's more than just a story.

Stanley (*only mildly enthusiastic*) Right. Excellent. Now, you are doing a little bit of exam revision as well I hope, Warren?

Warren Oh, yes, Mr Inchbridge ...

Stanley Not just working on these games? And stories? Splendid as they may be.

Warren No. I've been revising my notes every day. (*He indicates the envelope*) But I think that could change things, Mr Inchbridge. Change things as we perceive them now.

Stanley Yes, I do hope you are revising, Warren, because, as I said, you're not going to get there without a good bit of effort ...

Warren I am. I promise. I am.

Hazel enters, speaking as she enters. During the following, she lays a small cloth on the table and takes a couple of mats and a cruet from the sideboard

Hazel ... I mean I do, I worry about that child, I do. She's all alone in that great big house. I mean, her mother just left her there, didn't she? Just took off with that — man of hers — with not so much as a postcard — left the poor kid to fend for herself. I mean, I think that woman should have been prosecuted, I really do. Her own daughter ...

Hazel goes out again

Stanley (*calling after her, ineffectually*) That was years ago, Hazel, it's under the bridge ... (*To Warren*) What I'm saying is, Warren, if you put as much effort and ingenuity into your exam results as you put into these games of yours, you'd end up with a scholarship to Cambridge.

Warren Yes, Mr Inchbridge. I don't want to go to Cambridge, Mr Inchbridge.

Stanley Well, anywhere you chose.

Warren I want to stay here.

Stanley You've got a good brain, Warren. It's a special brain. So use it well, lad.

Warren I will, Mr Inchbridge.
Stanley How's your mother?
Warren (*dully*) She's OK.
Stanley Keeping well, is she?
Warren Yes. I'll say good-night, then.
Stanley Yes, good-night, Warren.

Hazel comes hurrying back with a tray, speaking as she enters. On the tray are some sandwiches wrapped in clingfilm, and a mug of milk similarly covered. She lays these out on the table

Hazel ... I mean, God knows if she eats at all. I've never seen her eat. Have you ever seen her eat? I haven't. We've only her word for it she eats at all, haven't we?
Stanley Well, she's a grown woman now, Hazel. And that's all under the bridge, isn't it?
Hazel That's where she'll probably end up ...
Warren Good-night, Mrs Inchbridge.
Hazel She's got a permanent cold. Runny nose ... Good-night, Warren, see you next week.
Warren Right.
Stanley Well, I'm no longer her teacher. I've no authority over her, have I?
Hazel How's your mother, Warren?
Warren (*as before*) The same as usual.
Stanley I haven't taught her for five years.
Hazel Give her my best, won't you?
Warren Yes. Good-night, Mr Inchbridge.
Stanley Good-night, Warren.

Warren moves to leave

Austen enters, nearly colliding with Warren. Austen is about fifty, a thick-set man of great authority. There is little doubt as to who is in real charge in this household. This evening he has had a couple of drinks — just enough to make him merry. He still has on his scarf and overcoat, which he now starts to remove

Warren Sorry, Mr Skate.
Austen (*cheerfully*) All finished playing, have we?
Warren Good-night.

He goes

Austen (*calling after Warren*) How's Mother?

Warren (*off*) Still there.
Stanley I'll see you off, Warren.
Austen I hope I haven't disturbed the playmates.
Hazel Let me take your coat, Austen.

Stanley goes out

Austen hands Hazel his coat and scarf during the next

Austen Still, past their bedtime, I expect.
Hazel That boy worries me to death as well ...
Austen What did we meet tonight? Dragons? Demons?
Hazel Your sandwiches are there for you, Austen.
Austen Hobgoblins? There must have been hobgoblins.
Hazel A boy like that needs a father. Even one that drank himself to death.
Austen What? No hobgoblins? We're slipping, aren't we? Come along. Come along, now. Someone's slipping. No hobgoblins. What about elves, then?
Hazel (*indicating Austen's coat*) I'll hang this up.
Austen Gnomes? Pixies?
Hazel (*moving to exit*) Don't eat the clingfilm again, will you?

She goes out with his coat and scarf

Austen Fairies? Praties? Banshees? Nymphs? Sprites? Bogey-men? Incubi? No succubi? Ghosts? Dwarves? Imps? Spooks?

Hazel returns

Well, you do disappoint me.
Hazel I'll bet he eats all the wrong things as well. His skin's in a shocking state. (*She starts to take the clingfilm off the sandwiches*)
Austen What about trolls? Did you meet any trolls?
Hazel Do you want tea, Austen?
Austen Dear me. It all sounds very dull. Hardly worth going, by the sound of it. Leprechauns? No. Kelpies?
Hazel Or coffee?
Austen No. Vampires? Harpies? Lycanthropes?

Stanley comes in and similarly ignores Austen

Werewolves?
Hazel I presume that means neither. Coffee, Stanley?

Stanley No, I'll just take my book upstairs, thanks.

Austen What's that you're reading, then? *Bumper Book for Boys*, is it? *The Beano Annual*? *The Beezer*? *Wizard and Chips*?

Stanley I think I'll have an early night.

Hazel You'll probably go straight to sleep as well, won't you? Wish we could all do that ...

She goes out again

Stanley Right. (*He acknowledges the other man's presence for the first time*) Night, Austen.

Austen Hey, Stanley! Hey! Before you go up ...

Stanley What?

Austen A little question for you ...

Stanley Oh, no, not just now, Austen ...

Austen No, no. A brain-teaser. This is right up your street. It arose this evening at the club. A question of semantics, Stanley. I thought straight away, Stanley's the man to ask, he'll know. I said to them. I said, my brother-in-law's an English teacher. He'll know. He's an expert.

Stanley Can't it wait till the morning, Austen?

Austen You'll like this, it's a good one. Fugue.

Stanley I beg your pardon?

Austen The word fugue. You've heard of that?

Stanley Yes.

Austen Meaning?

Stanley Well — a piece of music that repeats on itself ... I don't know the technical term for it ...

Austen All right. Good. Fair enough. Now. Pay attention. What is the other meaning of the word fugue?

Stanley Other meaning?

Austen Yes.

Stanley Haven't the faintest idea.

Austen Oh, come on, Stanley. An English teacher. Come on. Fugue. Fugue. Surely?

Stanley (*irritably*) I'm saying, I don't know. All right, what does it mean, then? Presumably you know or you wouldn't be asking me, would you?

Austen Yes, I do know as it happens. But there's no point in me telling you, is there? That's not how you learn, is it, Stanley? How do we learn? We learn by looking it up for ourselves. That's surely what you teach your students, isn't it? When you're not on your hands and knees playing games with them ...

Stanley Please don't start that, Austen ...

Austen Look it up. That's how we learn. That's what gives a person their idiolect. Are you cognizant with that word, Stanley? Neither was I at one period in my life, but I looked it up. Idiolect. A person's own individual way of speaking, that's what it means. I'll give you that one for free.

Stanley Thanks very much. Good-night.

Hazel returns. She and Stanley talk over Austen, who booms on regardless

Hazel Do you want to take up a hot-water bottle, Stanley? I think it'll be a bit chilly up there. We didn't put the heating back up.

Stanley No, I won't need one. I may have a read in the bath, I'll see.

Hazel Don't take all the water if you do, will you? I think I'll have one myself tonight. It's the only thing that might help me relax ...

Stanley You should take a pill if you're tense ...

Hazel (*heading for the exit*) I can't take any more. I'm full of pills as it is ...

Austen I mean, I'm not a teacher, am I? I don't pretend to be a teacher. I'm just a humble member of Her Majesty's Customs and Excise. A mere VAT inspector. But that doesn't stop me looking up a new word every day. It's not part of my job but I'm interested. Whereas for an English teacher, I'd have thought that would have been rather important. Rather vital. Rather exigent, wouldn't you say? If you know what I mean by exigent. Do you know that word, Stanley?

Stanley goes out, followed by Hazel

Austen (*continuing to speak loudly after them, still seated and between bites of sandwich*) I mean, if I were to ask you to perform complex mental arithmetic, I'd understand your reluctance, Stanley. That's not your line, after all. Not your area. That's my area. And it's a skill that, despite this age of computers and calculators, I feel is important for an alert mind to master. It's another discipline, that's all it is. And a very pleasurable one. If I see a column of figures — say, 9543 plus 362 plus 1837 plus 59 — I can immediately say the total equals — (*the merest pause*) — 11811.

Hazel pops her head round the door

Hazel Have you got enough sandwiches there, Austen?

Austen (*ignoring her*) 11801, I beg your pardon. I do beg your pardon.

Hazel I'll be in the kitchen if you want anything.

She goes out again

Austen I mean, that's all I'm saying. Don't mind me. (*He continues to eat*)

The Lights go down on Austen slightly

> *In the basement area, Rick lets herself in via the area door and switches on the light. Rick's house is silent and empty. Just the dripping of a distant tap. Occasional traffic passes above, the lights flashing briefly through her uncurtained windows*

> *After a moment, Austen goes off, leaving his empty plate and mug on the table*

Rick removes her motor-cycling gear and throws it carelessly in a corner. She locates a tin opener and, rummaging in a carrier on the floor, produces a tin (possibly of soup or vegetables), which she opens. She finds a spoon, which she wipes on her shirt, and then, seating herself, silently eats the contents of the tin

Suddenly from upstairs we hear the sound of a woman's footsteps scurrying across the floor. Rick glances up briefly, then resumes her meal. Silence

The Lights fade down on her slightly ...

... and come up on Warren's attic area, initially unlit apart from the glow from some of his permanently powered-up technical equipment

> *The trap door opens and Warren's head appears through the hole. He climbs through the trap door. As he does so, we hear his mother's voice from below. Presumably Thelma is standing at the foot of the loft ladder. We see very little of her. Occasionally she ventures up the ladder to her son's eyrie, but only the top of her head will be visible when she does, revealing a woman invariably dressed in black with brightly dyed red hair and with the small eyes and coarse features of a very large person indeed. It is doubtful whether she would even fit through the trap door. At this stage, all we will hear of her is her voice*

Thelma (*off*) ... Warren ... Is that you, Warren?
Warren Yes, Mother, it's me. Who else?
Thelma (*off*) Are you going to come down and have a cup of tea?
Warren I'm a bit busy just now, Mother.
Thelma (*off*) I've just made a cup ...
Warren No, thank you.
Thelma (*off, coaxingly*) Lovely nice cup of tea.
Warren No, thanks. I have things to do, Mother ...
Thelma (*off*) Cocoa. Lovely delicious hot cup of cocoa, then.

Warren No, thank you, Mother. I've got my revision.
Thelma (*off*) I'll make you a cocoa. Lovely hot nice delicious cup of ——

Warren closes the trap door before his mother can complete her sentence. He removes his anorak and hangs it up neatly. He sits at his console and switches on the computer screen. He closes his eyes and raises his hands, palms outermost

Warren (*in a strange voice*) It cannot be long now. It cannot be much longer, Arnie. (*He opens his eyes. He stares at the screen, then, after a second, starts to type furiously*)

The Lights cross-fade back to Rick, who is finishing her "supper". She sits motionless at the table. The tap continues to drip

From upstairs a man's heavy footsteps cross the floor above her head. A door slams somewhere overhead. We hear another set of footsteps — a woman's this time, then voices raised but muffled. Rick glances up briefly but doesn't move or react. She merely sits listening

Ken's voice Where the bloody hell is she? I want to know where she is?
Pat's voice Why don't you leave the kid alone, Ken? Just leave her alone.
Ken's voice When I find her she's in trouble, I can tell you that. She's in real trouble this time. I'm not having any kid of mine cheeking me like that ...
Pat's voice She's not your kid, is she? She's nothing to do with you, is she ...?
Ken's voice I'm living here. She's my responsibility while I'm in this house and she'll bloody well do as she's told, even if I have to thrash the daylights out of her. (*He yells*) Alice! Alice! Come on, I know you're hiding. Alice! You come here this second and eat your tea, do you hear me? Alice! (*His voice recedes*)
Pat's voice (*following him*) Ken, please! Ken, don't please! Just leave the bloody kid alone, why can't you ...?

Their footsteps move away. There is another distant door-slam. There is a silence. Rick continues to sit motionless

The Lights cross-fade back to the Inchbridges' sitting-room. The lights are still on though the room is empty. The distant sound of a water tank refilling

Hazel puts her head round the door, sees Austen's empty mug and plate and, coming into the room, clears and tidies the table. She is now in her nightclothes

Austen (*off*) Good-night, then. Don't dream of ghosts.

Hazel Good-night, Austen dear. Sleep well. (*She finishes her task, gives a final look around the room, gives a little shiver of unhappiness and switches off the lights*)

Hazel exits

The Lights return to Warren, who has paused in his typing to read what he has written. As he does this, there is a discreet knocking at the trap door in the floor

Thelma (*off, her voice muffled*) Warren ... Warren. Here's your cocoa ...

Warren scowls but chooses to ignore her

There is more insistent knocking

Warren. Warren, dear ...

Warren Hallo?

Thelma (*off*) It's your cocoa, dear. I've brought you up your cocoa.

Warren It's open. Just leave it there. Thank you, Mother.

The trap door is opened cautiously. Thelma's hand appears with a mug of steaming cocoa

Thelma (*off*) Here you are, dear. It's lovely and hot.

Warren (*without taking his eyes from the screen*) Thank you.

Thelma (*off*) I'm putting it just here. All right?

Warren Thank you.

Thelma (*off*) Don't let it go cold, will you?

Warren No.

Thelma (*off*) Drink it while it's hot.

Warren Yes.

Thelma (*off*) Don't be too late, will you, dear?

Warren No.

Thelma (*off*) Don't sit in front of those screens too long, will you?

Warren No.

Thelma (*off*) You know what happened to Mrs Chambers. Looking at screens for too long.

Warren Yes.

Thelma (*off*) That's how she lost her baby.

Warren (*through gritted teeth*) I'm not having a baby, am I?

Thelma (*off*) Good-night, dear. Don't forget to say your prayers, will you?

Warren No. Good-night.
Thelma (*off*) God bless you. I'll say a little prayer for you as well, dear.
Warren Thank you, Mother.

The trap door closes. Warren rises and, crossing to the trap door, bolts it shut angrily. He stands for a moment, then, instead of returning to his console, sits on the bed. After a moment, he lies back and stares at the ceiling. He falls asleep during the following

Retaining this image, we add to it the Inchbridge house and the sitting-room in virtual darkness

> *Hazel comes in from the hall. She stands by the window, gazing out. She is lit by the street lamp outside*

Add to this scene the basement. Rick rises and takes off her boots and jeans. She climbs into bed in just her pants and T-shirt and snuggles down under the uncovered duvet like a small child, with just her eyes showing. A man's footsteps are heard overhead

Ken's voice (*calling, coaxingly*) Alice! Alice! Alice!

Rick lies there with the light on

Hold all three images, then fade down to just the Inchbridges' sitting-room

> *Stanley, in pyjamas and dressing gown, looks round the door and sees Hazel*

Stanley Oh, hallo. Coming to bed?
Hazel Yes, in a minute.
Stanley Wondered where you were.
Hazel I was ... (*her voice tails away*)
Stanley You all right? (*He moves closer to her*) Hazel? All right?
Hazel Not really, no. If you want to know. No. (*She is crying*)
Stanley Hazel? What is it, old love?
Hazel Everything really. Us. (*She attempts a smile*) Life.
Stanley Well, yes. That's always worth a cry, is life. Anything special, though? Anything more to cry about than usual, is there?
Hazel I just looked at the four of us this evening, playing that game. Pretending to be people we weren't. Could never be, any of us. Not in our wildest dreams. I thought, oh dear, that's sad, isn't it? Just looking at us all. Two strange kids with no friends of their own except this daft, batty middle-aged couple.

Stanley Well, it's just a bit of fun, isn't it? It's not hurting anybody.

Hazel I think Austen's right, sometimes. We all ought to be put away.

Stanley No, Austen is never right. That's the only thing I know for certain in this world, Hazel. Austen can never be right. Even when he's right, he's wrong, that I do know. So don't go by him.

Hazel But what are we doing, Stanley? We can't play games all our lives, can we? Can we? Tell me. What do we both think we're doing?

Stanley We're — I think I'm teaching at Whinnythrop Lane and trying to shed a little light here and there to all those young eager minds — some of them — and I think you're ——

Hazel I'm —? What?

Stanley You're — well, I think you're working for the building society ——

Hazel Which I don't enjoy ...

Stanley Which you don't enjoy ...

Hazel Which I hate every minute of ...

Stanley Which you hate every minute of, but you'd never think of leaving, would you?

Hazel What if I did? What else is there for me to do?

Stanley Well ——

Hazel Stay home and look after you and Austen? More than I do already?

Stanley Not — necessarily ...

Hazel Well, what else? What else?

Stanley I don't know. Maybe we should ... Maybe we should try and have more fun. Do things together more. More holidays. Little ones. Needn't be that expensive. I mean, we could take weekend breaks. And go for walks. Things like that. Get the old tent out of the attic, why not? Be a laugh, wouldn't it? Go tenting again. Remember the laughs we had? (*He chuckles*)

Hazel sobs loudly

Hazel, come on. Come on, old love. Just tell me what'd you'd like most. Tell me what you want, we'll try and arrange it ...

Hazel (*uncontrollably*) I don't know what I want, do I?

Stanley (*miserably*) I'm sorry you're like this. I hate to see you like this. I'm sorry.

Hazel I'm sorry.

Stanley No. I'm sorry. I don't quite know what to do for the best, Hazel. I'm sorry.

Hazel I'm sorry ...

They stand close together, not touching. Silence

The Lights come up on the basement and the attic

Warren is now asleep on his bed

Rick lies under her duvet, still wide awake. There is a sudden loud knocking at her front door upstairs. Rick reacts, sits up slightly and listens. The knock is repeated, urgently. Rick remains frozen, listening

Hazel Don't worry, I'll snap out of it, don't worry. You know I get like this sometimes. Don't worry. Go to bed. I'll be up in a second.

Stanley remains where he is, looking at her

I shouldn't get like this. It's very selfish of me. I shouldn't let it get on top of me like this. I mean, you get depressed, I know you do. But you never burden other people with it, that's the difference. You're considerate. You keep it to yourself.

Stanley I'm all right. No bother about me.

Hazel You're not all right. Don't say you are. I see you sometimes. I notice.

Stanley Me? When?

Hazel I've seen you. I've noticed.

Stanley What?

Hazel Well, with Austen. He upsets you terribly sometimes, I know he does.

Stanley Nah! Not any more. He used to.

Hazel Why do you let him walk all over you? Why don't you stand up for yourself? He'd soon stop once you did. He's a bully, that's all he is. You should talk back at him sometimes.

Stanley I don't want to talk back at him. I don't want to talk to him at all.

Hazel He — belittles you. That's what he does. And in front of those kids.

Stanley Warren and Rick?

Hazel Yes.

Stanley They don't care. They've got the measure of Austen. Don't worry about them.

Hazel I'm not, I'm worrying about you.

Stanley I'm all right. I'm not the one who's standing here crying in the dark, am I?

Hazel You know what I'm talking about.

Stanley I haven't the faintest.

Hazel You know. (*She pauses*) You know.

There is a rattling at Rick's basement door. Rick sits up, alarmed

Marcie (*off; her voice comes through the door*) Rick? Rick? Are you in there! Rick!

There is more rattling at the door. Rick gets out of bed and cautiously moves to the door

Rick Who is it?
Marcie (*off*) Rick? Is that you?
Rick Who's that?
Marcie (*off*) It's me. Marcie. Please let me in, Rick. Please.
Rick (*reluctantly*) Just a minute.

Rick opens the door to admit Marcie. She is in her early twenties, attractive in a fresh, "untouched" sort of way. Her normal manner is to give whoever she is with her total, undivided, eager attention — an attractive quality, especially for the majority, who yearn for such a thing. At present Marcie seems a little breathless and flustered. Or at least as breathless and flustered as she can ever become

Marcie Hallo. Can I come in? It's important.
Rick (*closing the door after her*) What's wrong?
Marcie I'm ... (*breathlessly*) I'm ... Look, may I use your loo?
Rick (*indicating*) Yes, along there.
Marcie Would you mind awfully?
Rick Just along there.
Marcie Thanks.

Marcie hurries off further into the basement area

Rick stares after her, frowning slightly

Hazel We should have had children of our own. That's what we should have done.
Stanley Oh, come on. Not this again ——
Hazel We should.
Stanley Hazel, we've talked this ——
Hazel We could have moved away from here. Got our own place — instead of being lodgers like this.
Stanley We're not lodgers. This house is half yours ——
Hazel Lodgers. You know we are. He never lets us forget it. If Mary had lived she'd never have let us stay. She'd have found a way to get us out. She'd have persuaded Austen to buy us out if necessary.
Stanley (*a fraction out of patience*) Well, she's dead and we're here and he's here and we haven't got children and it's too late now and it's half-past twelve and we'd better make the best of it, hadn't we?

Warren wakes with a jolt. He gets off his bed and creeps to the trap door, unbolts it carefully and, opening it, looks down below. After a brief glance, he starts to descend, closing the trap door behind him

Hazel (*after a pause*) No. We should have had children. My mistake. Nothing to do with you. All my fault.

Stanley You used to say you didn't want them ...

Hazel That's what I used to say. I know I did. Well, I was wrong, wasn't I? I see now, I was wrong.

Stanley (*with a sigh*) Oh, dear. (*He moves away from her and sits*)

Hazel You should have made me, Stanley. You should have made me have them.

Stanley (*wearily*) What are you talking about?

Hazel You shouldn't have listened to me. You should have just — taken me by force. Forced me to have them.

Stanley Oh, Hazel ...

Hazel You think you can beat her — but you never do. She'll get you eventually. She always does. She knows.

Stanley Who are we talking about now?

Hazel Nature. Bloody old Mother Nature. She knows. You think you can outsmart her, but you never can. She gets her revenge in the end.

Stanley Hazel, it's quarter to one, old love.

Marcie returns. She has tidied herself and now looks almost pristine again — her normal appearance

Rick stares at her

Marcie Oh, that's better. Thank you. I didn't know what I was going to do. I was frantic. I thought, where can I go? Who do I know who can help? And then I thought of you, Rick, I hope you don't mind. I remembered I'd taken your address at work. You remember? When we were all of us going to that concert and then you didn't come? Remember? I hope you didn't mind, Rick. I was just so desperate.

There is a slight pause

Rick To use my toilet, you mean?

Marcie What? Oh, no.

Rick No?

Marcie Well, only incidentally. No. It's Larry.

Rick Larry?

Marcie My husband. He — I left him. Tonight. He started hitting me — punching ...

Rick Punching you?

Marcie Yes. I've got bruises all up my arms — I'll show you if you don't believe me — I always knew he was violent, Rick. Potentially. I mean, he's been in trouble in the past, but I never thought he'd hit me. Not me. He loved me — he said he loved me — but tonight he just — came at me — just wild — trying to hit my face — I don't know what I said — I can't think of anything I could have done to make him like that — I covered my head (*she demonstrates*) like this — that's how he bruised my arms. It was terrifying, Rick, just terrifying. No one's ever — ever hit me before. Ever. I was so frightened. I just ran out of the house — just as I was. Like this. (*She pauses for breath*)

Rick stares at her

Do you — do you have — anything to drink?

Rick What, you mean like — whisky?

Marcie No. Coffee. Anything.

Rick Tea.

Marcie Lovely.

Rick Bag.

Marcie Naturally.

Rick No milk.

Marcie Just a teeny drop.

Rick No, there isn't any.

Marcie Oh right. Perfect.

Rick exits, leaving Marcie to stare round the room somewhat critically. She sits at the table

Hazel (*who has reached a new low*) I sometimes catch myself staring at myself in that bathroom mirror and I think — what have you done with that body, Hazel? What have you done with it, woman? You've wasted it. That's what you've done. Look at it. Shrivelling and drooping and wasting away — covered in brown spots and warts and wrinkles and what use have you ever made of it? Nothing. It's not even produced children.

Stanley (*muttering*) There are other things, aren't there?

Hazel (*sharply*) What? What did you say?

Stanley I said there are other things besides children.

Hazel What? What else is there? For a woman? That's what we were designed for. What else use are we?

Stanley Oh, come on, Hazel, now you're being stupid.

Hazel I should have done what my mother did. That's all she did. All her life. Had children and looked after them all her life. That was the natural thing. And she was happy doing it.

Stanley What are you talking about? She was as miserable as hell.
Hazel She wasn't.
Stanley She was the most miserable woman I've ever met.
Hazel Nonsense.
Stanley She was, Hazel. I remember her.
Hazel Only — only towards the end. Most of her life she wasn't. She was only unhappy at the end.
Stanley Yes, because she realized she'd wasted her whole bloody life looking after you and Austen.
Hazel At least she had us. What have I got?
Stanley (*muttering*) Me.
Hazel What?
Stanley I said me. You've got me.

There is a silence

Hazel, it's quarter past one.

Warren emerges again through his trap door. He has made himself an enormous white-bread doorstep sandwich, already half eaten. His cheeks are bulging. He closes the trap door and rebolts it. He sits back on the bed and eats

Hazel I've wasted this body. I haven't even given pleasure with it.
Stanley You did to me ...
Hazel No, I didn't. I just lay there. Like a plank. Rigid. I was terrified of the whole business.
Stanley Well, that's various things. Me among them. It was probably me. Most probably, looking back. I don't know.
Hazel No. It was my fault. I should have put you at your ease. That's what a woman's meant to do. That's her job.
Stanley It's nobody's job. It's not a job, Hazel. Sex isn't a job. It's supposed to be — spontaneous — and effortless — and easy.
Hazel If it's that easy, why do they need to write all these books explaining it to people? Tell me that. No, it was me. My mother told me once my father used to play her like a violin every night of her married life ... That's never happened to us.
Stanley (*muttering*) What did you want me to do? Tuck you under my chin?
Hazel (*sharply*) What?
Stanley Nothing.
Hazel Don't make jokes about it, Stanley, please. Don't joke about it.
Stanley Maybe we should, Hazel. Maybe that's the trouble.
Hazel It's nothing to joke about, is it? Surely? No, I think if you want to know,

that's been our trouble half the time. I mean — how can you seriously love someone if they keep laughing?

Stanley I have no answer to that, Hazel.

Hazel Look at the time, it's twenty to two. What are we doing?

Stanley No idea at all.

Hazel You all right?

Stanley No. If you want to know. Not all. I'm very depressed.

Hazel Oh, don't you start. Just because I do. One of us is enough.

Stanley Maybe it's connected, Hazel.

Hazel I'll make a bottle. (*She moves to the door*) Are you staying down? Don't stay down too long, will you?

Hazel exits

Stanley sits gloomily in his chair

Rick returns with two mugs of black tea; the tea-bags are still in them

Rick Here.

Marcie Lovely.

Rick Sorry it took so long. That electric kettle's faulty. You have to hold the switch in while it boils.

Marcie Oh dear. You ought to get it mended.

Rick Yes.

Marcie You could always boil water in a saucepan whilst it was being fixed.

Rick Saucepan?

Marcie Yes.

Rick I don't have any saucepans.

Marcie No saucepans?

Rick No. No point. I don't have a stove.

Marcie What do you cook on, then?

Rick I don't cook.

Marcie What do you eat?

Rick Cold.

Marcie All the time?

Rick Or take-away.

Marcie Oh. (*She removes her tea-bag with difficulty*) Where shall I — ? With this?

Rick Anywhere. Doesn't matter.

Marcie (*putting it as tidily as she can on the table*) I'll put it here.

Rick Fine.

Hazel puts her head round the sitting-room door. She clutches a hot-water bottle

Hazel (*softly*) Stanley ...
Stanley Mmm?
Hazel Come on upstairs now, dear. It's nearly two o'clock.
Stanley Coming ...

Hazel gives a worried look at her husband and exits. In a moment, Stanley follows

Marcie Is this ... (*She indicates the room*) Is this — just a temporary arrangement, or do you ... ?
Rick What?
Marcie Or do you live here all the time? I mean, I was only asking, don't ——
Rick No, this is — sort of permanent. Home, you know.
Marcie Who else lives here, then?
Rick How do you mean?
Marcie In this house. Who lives upstairs?
Rick Nobody. It's empty.
Marcie You mean you have the whole house to yourself?
Rick Yes.
Marcie How lucky. Who owns it, then?
Rick Me.
Marcie What?
Rick I do.
Marcie You own this house? All of it.
Rick Yes.
Marcie Then — excuse my asking, but why do you live down here? In the basement? It's a huge house. You could live up there, couldn't you? Surely?
Rick No.
Marcie Why not?
Rick (*slightly tense*) Because I prefer it down here.

There is a slight pause

Marcie How did you get it?
Rick What?
Marcie The house? How do you come to own it?
Rick It was — left to me ...
Marcie Who by?
Rick My mother and ... My parents ...
Marcie Are they both dead, then?
Rick No. They left.

Marcie When did they leave?
Rick (*vaguely*) Oh. Years ago.
Marcie I see. (*She is definitely intrigued*) I never realized you were ...
Well, of course, you don't get time to talk properly. Not at work. One's
too busy ... serving people and——
Rick Washing up.
Marcie Exactly.

From upstairs comes the sound of the front-door knocker. They jump

What's that?
Rick Front door. Upstairs.

More knocking

Larry (*his muffled voice*) Marcie! Marcie! Are you in there? Marcie!
Marcie (*breathlessly*) It's Larry.
Rick How does he know you're here?
Marcie I don't know. He must have — Oh, my God! He mustn't get in.

More knocking

Rick I'll turn out the light. (*She does so*)

There is darkness, except for light through the windows

Marcie (*whispering*) What if he gets in?
Rick He can't get in, don't worry.

*A shadow falls across the room from outside as Larry comes down the area
steps*

Marcie (*rising and backing to a far corner; a stifled scream*) Oh, no ...
Rick Sssh!

The door handle rattles

Larry (*off*) Marcie. I know you're in there somewhere, Marcie. Don't think
you can hide from me because you can't. (*He pauses*) Marcie? I'll only be
back, Marcie. I'll find you sooner or later, so why not come home now,
there's a good girl. (*He pauses*) Marcie?

Larry hovers for a moment, then the shadow recedes and we hear footsteps going back up the steps

Marcie Thank heavens.
Rick Shh! Make sure he's gone.

They wait a second or so

OK. Safe now. Better leave the lights off for a bit, though.
Marcie Would you — would you mind if I just lay down for a second? I feel ... I feel a bit ...
Rick Sure. Use the bed. There. Use my bed.
Marcie Thanks. Are you sure ——?
Rick Fine. Why don't you get some sleep? You look as if you need sleep. It's all right, I've got another bed. Use that one.
Marcie Thank you. (*She approaches the bed, examines it rather suspiciously, then decides she has little other choice*) You don't — you don't have a spare nightie, do you? (*She looks at Rick*) No. 'jamas? No?
Rick Sorry.
Marcie Oh, well, doesn't matter. What the hell. All girls together, aren't we? (*She undresses, finally stripping down to her bra and pants*)

Rick watches Marcie intently

(*Unaware of Rick's attention*) Just for a second then, I was so frightened. Terrified, you've no idea. I don't know what he'd have done if he'd got in. He'd probably have tried to kill me or something. Both of us. He has this terrible temper, you can't imagine. He nearly went to prison for attacking a man in a betting shop. That was long before he met me, of course ... (*She becomes aware of Rick's gaze*) What's the matter?
Rick (*looking away from Marcie*) Nothing.

During the next, Marcie folds up her outer garments neatly on the chair and finally climbs into bed and snuggles under the duvet

Marcie He might have killed me, the mood he was in tonight.
Rick He'd've had to deal with me first.
Marcie Well. Possibly. But he's very powerful — I'm going to be an absolute slug tonight, I'm not even going to wash — he used to pick me up sometimes as if I were two stone. He's incredibly strong.
Rick So am I.
Marcie (*slightly doubtful*) Really? But not ——
Rick And I'm trained.

Marcie Trained?
Rick Unarmed combat. Don't worry. I can take care of myself.
Marcie Does it work?
Rick What?
Marcie Unarmed combat?
Rick Of course it works.
Marcie Oh. I sometimes wondered. You hear these stories ——
Rick I could bring a fourteen-stone man to his knees with a broken nose in
three and a half seconds.
Marcie (*sleepily*) Golly. That'd teach him.
Rick I could break his marriage vows with the toe of my boot. Don't worry.
You're safe here.
Marcie (*impressed*) That's nice to hear, anyway. (*She is suddenly drowsy*)
At least I'm in good ... (*She yawns*) ... At least I'm in good ... (*she yawns
again*) ... sorry ... hands ...

*Rick stands looking at the sleeping figure. Then she gently brushes Marcie's
hair from her eyes, adjusts the duvet more snugly around her and finally,
spreading out her anorak, curls up at the foot of the bed like a protective dog*

The Lights fade on all areas

Scene 2

The same. A week later

*Both Warren's attic and Rick's basement are empty and unlit. The lights are
on at the Inchbridges', though*

*Hazel hurries in, wearing an apron, her fist full of cutlery. She looks rather
distraught. Stanley follows anxiously, carrying the anglepoise lamp*

Hazel (*as she enters*) ... I mean, I've barely finished feeding you and Austen
and then we've got those two arriving ...
Stanley It's all right, old love, there's no hurry. No hurry.
Hazel (*replacing the cutlery in the sideboard drawer*) ... I mean, I wouldn't
mind a little time to myself, I really wouldn't. Just occasionally ...
Stanley Well, all right, we'll try and arrange that, then. We'll see what we
can arrange ...
Hazel I mean, no wonder I look about a hundred and ten ...

Hazel exits

Stanley (*feebly*) You look — fine ...

But Hazel has gone. Stanley sighs, clamps the anglepoise to the table and switches it on

The doorbell rings

Hazel (*off; a cry from the kitchen*) Oh, no ...
Stanley (*hastily*) It's all right, I'll go, old love. I'll go.

Stanley hurries out. We hear him admitting Warren

Warren (*off*) Evening, Mr Inchbridge.
Stanley (*off*) Good-evening, Warren. Come in, come in.

Stanley ushers Warren into the room

Shan't be a moment, we're just a little ——
Warren (*glancing round*) Not too early, am I?
Stanley No, no. Well, maybe a fraction. Not to worry, Warren. Let me take your coat.
Warren Thank you, Mr Inchbridge. Only I wondered if we'd be able to get a quiet word about "I, an Alien".

Stanley goes out momentarily to hang up Warren's anorak as he says the following

Stanley I beg your pardon?
Warren About my statement, "I, an Alien". Did you read it?

Stanley returns

Stanley Oh yes. Yes, I did. It's fascinating, Warren. Very imaginative. Extraordinary.
Warren It's all based on scientific fact.
Stanley Well — scientific conjecture, I think would be nearer the mark, Warren. I mean to say, we don't have concrete proof that there are aliens actually living among us. Not at this present time. Of course, it could be that you're right and they're here, there and everywhere even as we speak ——
Warren I am right, Mr Inchbridge.
Stanley Possibly. All I'm saying is that we have no proof, though, do we?
Warren I do, Mr Inchbridge.

Stanley Now, that's not technically correct, is it?

Warren I'm proof. I am an alien, Mr Inchbridge.

Stanley No, now ...

Warren What more proof do you want? It's all here.

Stanley No. I think what you're experiencing, Warren, is what they call alienation. Which is not altogether uncommon, especially at your age, but it's still very different from being an alien.

Warren Yes, but the word alienation — where does that come from in the first place, Mr Inchbridge?

Stanley Well, presumably, yes, from the word alien. Granted.

Warren Exactly. Now, according to Arnie Van der Hooch ...

Stanley Who?

Warren (*excitedly*) The man whose book I've based that on. We are not one race at all. There is no such thing as mankind as such, Mr Inchbridge. We are, in fact, formed from seven or maybe eight different inter-galactic species, part of an exploratory expedition that crash-landed here half a million years ago and caused the Grand Canyon.

Stanley Now, Warren, that is just conjecture ....

Warren It isn't, not at all. Why do you think people are different colours?

Stanley Now, there are reasons for that. This is nonsense.

Warren (*triumphantly*) Then why do you think women are so different from men, Mr Inchbridge? Answer me that?

There is a pause. Stanley is stumped for a reply

Stanley (*gently*) Have you — have you talked to your mother about this, Warren?

Warren (*sulkily*) How can I talk to her? She's an Orgue.

Stanley An Orgue?

Warren They're a lower life form. They only brought them along as labour. For menial duties.

The doorbell rings

Stanley (*worriedly*) Excuse me, Warren, I'll be back in a minute. Just a minute.

Stanley goes out

Warren (*unhappily*) He was right. Nobody ever believes it.

Rick (*off*) Evening, Mr Inchbridge ...

Stanley (*off*) Hallo, Rick, come in ... Oh, who have we here?

Marcie (*off*) Good-evening, Mr Inchbridge, I'm Marcie Banks. I'm a friend of Rick's, I hope you don't mind ...

Stanley (*off, uncertainly*) No, no. Not at all. Come in, please.
Marcie (*off*) Thank you.

A second later Stanley ushers in Marcie and Rick. They are both clad in motor-cycle kit and carrying their helmets

Stanley Do come in. Please come through. This is Warren Wrigley, a pupil of mine ...
Marcie (*beaming at Warren*) Hallo, Warren ...
Stanley This is — er — I've forgotten your name again ...
Marcie Marcie. Marcie Banks.
Warren (*gaping at her, totally smitten; he continues to stare at her during the following*) Ur.
Stanley Marcie's a friend of Rick's, Warren.
Marcie We work together.
Stanley Oh, do you? At the ——
Marcie At the Potty Shrimp. We call it that, anyway. I'm a waitress.
Stanley Oh. How interesting.

There is a silence

Marcie Isn't this lovely? What a lovely room.
Stanley Yes. Thank you. Let me take your — things ...
Marcie (*beaming at him*) Thank you, Mr Inchbridge.
Stanley (*rapidly succumbing to her charms as well*) Stanley — Stanley, if you'd prefer ...
Marcie Right. Thank you.

Stanley takes Rick's and Marcie's gear from them. As he is doing this, there is a crash of breaking crockery from the kitchen and an accompanying wail from Hazel. Stanley reacts

Stanley Just a moment, please, I'll see what the problem is. Talk among yourselves. Perhaps you'd like to lay things out, Warren.
Warren (*who hasn't taken his eyes off Marcie*) Right, Mr Inchbridge.

Stanley goes out

Marcie (*turning her attention to Warren, brightly*) Rick tells me you're a computer wizard. Is that right, Warren?
Warren (*muttering, embarrassed*) I know a bit about them.

During the next, Warren gets the game board and pieces from the sideboard and sets them out. Marcie watches him; Rick stands awkwardly by

Marcie I wish I did. I took a course once but I couldn't come to terms with them at all. They frighten me to death. They just sit there whirring at you. I'm terrified I'll press the wrong button and they'll blow up. Crash or whatever they do.

Warren (*muttering inaudibly*) It's difficult to blow them up.

Marcie Sorry?

Warren (*a fraction louder*) They're very difficult to blow up.

Marcie So they say. You don't know me.

Warren starts to set out the board

Ah! This must be the famous game?

Warren Yes.

Marcie Which you invented?

Warren Yes.

Marcie Hey, genius!

Warren (*warming a little*) Well, in a way. It's based on a standard role-playing game which I update and up-program every week, thus allowing the computer to select and print out variable parameters and random options as and when we require them.

Marcie (*flatly*) No, I don't understand a single word of that. Rick tells me you play every week?

Warren Yes.

Marcie How nice. And these are all your little people?

Warren Yes.

Marcie Which one's you?

Warren (*pointing to Xenon*) That one.

Marcie Eeek! Terrifying, what is it?

Warren That's Xenon. He's the alien. He's from the planet Lakkos.

Marcie Wouldn't like to meet him on a dark night.

Warren (*warming up further*) Oh, no. The Laks are known to be extremely friendly and gentle. On Lakkos they're highly civilized. They have advanced sight and hearing. They can hear music from the Milky Way.

Marcie I love his face. Why did you chose him?

Warren (*evasively*) I — just did.

Marcie (*smiling at him*) That's fascinating. I'd love to know why.

Rick (*suddenly, breaking this up*) That's me, there. Herwin. The Warrior.

Marcie (*picking up Idonia*) This one? Oh, she's beautiful.

Rick (*irritably*) No, not that one. That's Idonia — that's Hazel — Mrs Inchbridge. This one. That's Herwin. That's me.

Marcie Wow! Now you're talking. Tough.

Rick Kills anything in her path. Half woman, half machine.

Marcie Golly. Idonia's a terribly pretty little girl, though, isn't she? (*She picks up the fourth figure*) And this one must be ...

Warren Mr Inchbridge. Alric, the Wise One.

As Warren speaks, Stanley enters with a couple of kitchen chairs

Stanley Sorry. Hazel's just coming. Ah, good, you've set it out. Splendid. Explaining it to Marcie? Now, Marcie, would you like to sit and watch or would you like to join in?
Marcie Well ...
Rick She only came to watch.
Warren She can play if she wants to ...
Marcie Would that be all right?
Stanley Yes, of course it will. Warren, fetch another chair, would you?
Warren Yes, Mr Inchbridge. (*He heads for the door*)

Hazel enters at the same moment

Rick (*to Marcie*) I thought you only wanted to watch?
Marcie Well, it looks such fun.
Hazel What's going on? Where are you going, Warren?
Warren Fetching another chair, Mrs Inchbridge.
Hazel We've got enough, surely?

Warren goes out

Stanley Marcie's going to join the game, Hazel. Hazel, this is Marcie. Marcie, my wife, Hazel.
Marcie How do you do, Mrs Inchbridge.
Hazel (*distracted*) How do you do. (*Then, ignoring Marcie, to Stanley*) I don't see how she can, we're half-way through a game.
Stanley Well, Marcie can be a character we've met on the way. We're always meeting people on the way.
Hazel Yes, but they don't all join us ...
Stanley No, but this one could have done ...
Hazel They don't all tag along, willy-nilly, do they? I mean, if they all joined us there'd hundreds of them. Innkeepers and hunchbacks and God-knows-what ...
Stanley Yes, but in this case ...
Hazel Woodcutters ... distressed damsels ...

Warren enters with another chair during the next

Stanley Yes, but they didn't have anyone to control them. To play them. Now, there's Marcie ...
Marcie Look, I can just as easily sit and watch if it's a problem ...

Stanley It's no problem. Is it, Warren?

Warren No problem.

Stanley Rick?

Rick (*rather sourly*) Do what you like.

Hazel She hasn't even got a piece. She's going to need a piece, a figurine.

Stanley We can give her something temporarily. Just for this week. Anything will do. I know, give her a bit of the cruet, that will do for now.

Hazel (*getting the cruet from the sideboard*) I still think it's very odd indeed.

Stanley We can get her something more suitable for next week — assuming she'll be back next week. Can we hope to see Marcie with you regularly, Rick ...?

Rick ... er ...

Marcie (*smiling at Rick*) I hope so.

Rick Yes.

Hazel Have you a preference for salt or pepper, Marcie?

Marcie Whichever's most convenient, Mrs Inchbridge.

Hazel Salt, then.

Stanley Now, we must work you out a character, Marcie. Warren? That's usually Warren's department. He's the brains behind the game.

Warren She can be Novia. The Newcomer.

Marcie That's a lovely name, thank you.

Stanley Right. Down with the lights. On with the game. (*He switches off the overheads. The board is now illuminated by just the anglepoise as before. He joins the others at the table*)

Hazel I don't think I can play for too long tonight. I've got so much to catch up with ...

Stanley Well, you just say when, Hazel. Now, do we have tonight's game parameters, Warren?

Warren (*fishing some computer print-out sheets from his pocket*) Got them here, Mr Inchbridge ...

Stanley Remind us where we were, will you? Get Xenon to remind us. (*To Marcie*) We always have a little recap at the start, Marcie, just to remind ourselves ...

Marcie Yes ...

Warren To the north are the Mountains of Ag and beyond that the Kingdom of Endocia, the Virgin Queen ——

Marcie Oh ...

Warren —— Ruler of the Fish people. To the west, the Kingdom of Orrich, Lord of all Oak Trees and the Forest of Emptiness.

Marcie Golly.

Warren To the east, the Grey River, which winds into the Valley of Disappointment and Despair.

Marcie Aah.

Warren And to the south there lie-eth the Dead Place. The land ruled over by Balaac, the Beast.

Marcie Wow!

Stanley Ah, yes. Of course. We had sighted the Kingdom of Balaac. He whom we had sought for so long, Balaac, the Evil One. Whom we had sworn, each of us for our own secret reason, to destroy. Balaac, the Beast, the reason for our banding together ...

Hazel Yes, we know this, Stanley ...

Warren Alric ...

Hazel We know this, Alric, O Wise One ...

Stanley I speak for the benefit of the fair Novia, the newest amongst us ... Welcome, child ...

Marcie Hallo, everyone ...

Hazel (*muttering at her*) Greetings. You're supposed to say greetings ...

Marcie Greetings, everybody ...

Warren We try and talk in old English ...

Stanley Sort of old English. Not genuine, of course. We'd never understand each other at all. But it helps to give it a bit of an atmosphere.

Marcie Oh, yes. Yea ...

Stanley So, friends, you have heard from Xenon, the Stranger. We must decide if we are yet strong enough to face the final challenge of Balaac, the Evil One. He whom we have sought these many years ... What say you, Idonia, Enchantress and Child of Many Tongues?

Hazel Strooch-snairt-hoooom-whereno-traays ...

Marcie (*whispering*) What did she say?

Warren (*sotto voce*) She's speaking in one of her many tongues.

Hazel Hoore-haaar. I say we should rest further before proceeding, O Wise One. The dangers are many and I see much travail.

Stanley Despite your youth, you speak wisely. Xenon?

Warren I, too, would advise caution, Alric. The hour is not yet ready. We should travel first to other lands to gain more wisdom and strength.

Stanley So be it. What say you, Herwin, the Silent One?

Rick (*who's more self-conscious than ever with Marcie there; muttering*) We should wait, O Wise One.

Stanley (*not hearing her*) What sayest thou, Herwin?

Rick (*louder*) I say, we should wait, Wise One.

Stanley So be it. Then it is the decision of Alric, your leader, that we should travel to the east and the ——

Marcie I don't think we should. I think we should go after old what's-his-name — Balaac, that's what I think.

There is a silence

Thinketh.

Hazel Be silent, Novia. It is not right to question the wisdom of Alric, our leader.

Stanley Nay, let the child have speech. What sayest thou, Novia, newest amongst us?

Marcie I think we should goeth after this Balaac now. While he's there. I mean, we're a pretty formidable collection, or so it seemeth to me. We haveth Herwin here, who is mighty and strong. And the mega-frightening-looking Xenon with all his powers. And the beautiful enchantress — Mrs ... sorry ——

Hazel Idonia.

Marcie — who is obviously bursting with magic. And then there's you, O Wise One. And me. What waiteth we for?

There is a stunned silence

Stanley Well ...

Hazel (*muttering*) It is not right that she question your decision, O Leader. She should be punished.

Stanley Yes, well, no. Let's consider her point ...

Hazel Your decision is final, O Leader. Thus is it writ.

Stanley (*dithering*) Well, yes, only ...

Warren Maybe she should be heard, O Leader. Maybe we should travel south ...

Hazel We can't travel south. You heard what Alric said ——

Warren Nay, but she is young and beautiful and I of a clear mind ...

Hazel Well, I'm sorry, I'm also young and beautiful and I have to say I think she's wrong ...

Stanley Nay, nay ...

Hazel And she's only just joined us and she should keep her mouth shut ...

Stanley Nay, Idonia child, this is not the way ...

Rick		I think we should go east, we're not ready to fight yet. She's only just joined us ...
Warren		No, I think she has a point. We should go south and risk it ...
Stanley	(*together*)	Now, now, now, now, now now ...
Marcie		Look, I really don't want to cause any trouble. I was only just putting in my suggestion ...
Hazel		She's made her suggestion and that's the end of it. Now we do what we decided to do in the first place ...

Stanley (*shouting them down*) Now wait, wait, wait! Please!

There is a silence

Alric speaks to you. Your leader speaks. If we quarrel amongst ourselves, we will surely perish. Therefore I will choose for us. And I have chosen. We will do as Novia, the Newcomer, suggests and travel south to meet Balaac.

Hazel Oh, that's ridiculous.

Stanley (*firmly*) Alric has spoken, child. The Old Wise One has chosen.

Hazel (*under her breath*) Oh, well, if we're going to start taking orders from a salt-cellar ...

Stanley (*ignoring this*) We are agreed, then, friends? Southwards to the Dead Place, ruled by Balaac himself?

Warren Balaac!

Marcie Balaac!

Hazel (*rather more reluctantly*) Balaac!

Rick (*likewise*) Balaac!

At this moment, Austen enters, switching on the lights as he does so. He stops as he sees the others sitting there, blinking in the sudden brightness

Austen Oh, it's you lot. I forgot about you.

Hazel Austen, why aren't you at your meeting?

Austen It was cancelled. Guest speaker taken ill at the last moment ... I hope you don't expect me to sit in the kitchen while you chase goblins ...?

Hazel (*rising*) No, no ...

Stanley (*also rising*) No, we'll — we'll pack in a bit early tonight, I think. We're all a bit tired.

Hazel (*removing the salt-cellar and replacing it in the sideboard*) Yes, I've got masses to get on with ...

Marcie Oh, what a shame.

Austen Hallo. What's this? A new recruit for the funny farm?

Stanley This is a friend of Rick's. Marcie, this is my brother-in-law, Austen, Marcie.

Marcie How do you do.

Austen (*looking at Marcie approvingly*) Well, well, well ...

Hazel I'll make your sandwiches, Austen. I haven't done them yet. Excuse me.

Hazel goes out

Stanley and Warren pack up the game and the anglepoise during the following

Rick immediately follows Hazel into the hall

Austen A friend of Rick's?

Marcie Yes, we work together, Mr ———?
Austen Skate, Austen Skate. Quite presentable, isn't she? Whatever next? (*He laughs*)

Marcie smiles, embarrassed

How come you know Rick?
Marcie Well, we work together, Rick and me.
Austen Rick and I, not Rick and me. Rick and I, young lady. There's an English teacher in the room, didn't you know? We must mind our p's and q's.
Marcie Yes, I'd ...
Austen Stanley's usually very strict about things like that. He can't have been listening. Thank your lucky stars, young lady. You might have got six of the best. (*He laughs, sits and starts to read his newspaper*)

Marcie smiles uncertainly. Stanley looks rather apologetic

Rick reappears in her motor-cycle gear, carrying her helmet and Marcie's

Rick You coming, then?
Marcie Oh, all right.
Stanley No, don't dash away. Stay for a while.
Marcie (*torn*) Well ...
Rick No, we have to be off. I need to get back.
Marcie Why?
Rick I need to be going.
Marcie We could stay for a little bit, couldn't we?
Stanley Please.
Rick Well, you can if you like. I have to go.
Marcie Well, all right ...
Rick You coming then?
Marcie No, you go. I'll see you later.

There is a slight pause

Rick (*uncertain*) Right. You'll have to walk.
Marcie That's OK. Can you take my helmet?
Rick 'night.
Warren 'night.
Stanley 'night.
Austen Good-night.

Rick leaves

Stanley Something wrong?
Marcie Sorry?
Stanley With Rick. She seems a bit — put out.
Marcie Really?

Warren has finished packing things away

Warren I'll be off too, Mr Inchbridge.
Stanley You can't stay either, Warren?
Warren No, I need to ... I have to ... Good-night, Mr Skate.
Austen (*in his paper*) Good-night, Warren. Don't get run over by a
   spaceship, will you?
Warren (*laughing hollowly*) Ha! Ha! Ha! Ha! Ha! I'll try not to, Mr Skate.
   Good-night — er ...
Marcie Good-night, Warren. (*She smiles*) It's a really great game. See you
   again soon, I hope.
Warren (*confused*) Yes. Probably.

Warren goes out

*Austen reads the paper. Stanley smiles at Marcie. Marcie smiles at Stanley.
There is a silence*

Marcie Sorry. It's just me, then. Do you want me to go?
Stanley No, no. After all, we ought to get to know you a bit, oughtn't we?
   I mean, you'd hardly walked through the door and you were dragooned
   straight into our game ...
Marcie Not really. I enjoyed it.
Stanley We normally play for hours but ...

*They are both very conscious of Austen, even though he's pointedly ignoring
them. Marcie smiles at Stanley. He smiles at her*

Austen Don't mind me. Don't mind me.
Stanley Would you like a cup of tea? Or something.
Marcie Thank you.

Hazel hurries in to lay the table, as before

Hazel Well, have they all ... ? (*She stops as she sees Marcie*) Oh, still here?
Marcie Yes.
Hazel Not gone with Rick?
Marcie No.

Hazel Oh. Well. Excuse me. (*She carries on with her tasks*)

Stanley We thought we might have a cup of tea.

Hazel We? Who's we?

Stanley Well, all of us.

Hazel All of us?

Stanley Yes.

Hazel I don't want a cup of tea, I haven't got time.

Stanley Ah.

Hazel Do you want a cup of tea, Austen?

Austen No, I don't want a cup of tea.

Hazel Right. It's just the two of you, then. Fine. Why didn't you say so in the first place?

Stanley I can do it.

Hazel (*heading for the exit*) It's no problem at all.

Hazel exits

Stanley She's — sometimes, my wife's a little ...

Marcie It's all right, I understand. She's like my mother gets ...

Stanley Ah. You live with your parents?

Marcie No. I ran away.

Stanley Oh.

Marcie To get married.

Stanley Ah. You're married.

Marcie Separated.

Stanley Oh.

Marcie Yes.

Stanley You've obviously crammed quite a lot into a short life.

Marcie Yes.

Austen (*in his paper*) Thirteen shopping days to Christmas. (*He looks up*) Don't mind me. Don't mind me.

There is a silence

Stanley Oh, Lord. Look. He's left his short story. Warren. He meant to take it.

Marcie I could drop it round to him sometime, if you like.

Stanley No, there's no problem. It can always wait till next week.

Marcie Please, I'll do it with pleasure. If you have his address.

Stanley Yes, I'll let you have it before you ——

There is a crash from the kitchen and a cry of irritation from Hazel

Austen Dear, dear, dear ...

Stanley Perhaps we'd better ... Look, would you mind having that tea in the kitchen ... ?

Marcie No, not at all. I'd love to see your kitchen, too.

Stanley It's nothing special ...

Marcie I love kitchens.

Austen Oh, Stanley ...

Stanley Yes?

Austen Did you ever look up that word I told you about?

Stanley Word?

Austen Fugue. Fugue, Stanley. Remember I said it had another meaning?

Stanley No, I didn't. Haven't had time.

Austen Well, I'll tell you. Since you are apparently an English teacher with a reluctance for some reason to consult a dictionary. Fugue can also mean a form of amnesia which is a flight from reality. Isn't that interesting?

Stanley Very.

Austen There you are, young lady, come to this house you can learn something new every day, can't you?

Marcie (*smiling sweetly*) You certainly can, Mr Skate, thank you.

Austen Don't mind me. Carry on.

Marcie and Stanley go out

The outside street lights come up on Rick's basement area as she comes in through her door, closes it and, during the next, lays down her cycle helmet and removes her jacket. She goes off further into the basement for a moment

Austen reads the paper

Hazel comes in with his sandwiches

Hazel (*putting the plate on the table*) There you are. (*She sits in the other chair*) I'll get you your cocoa. It's still very early.

Austen (*sitting*) What are you doing?

Hazel What?

Austen Sitting there? Why are you sitting down?

Hazel Why shouldn't I? Do you mind me sitting down?

Austen You never sit down.

Hazel Well, I feel a little in the way in there. Thought I'd better leave them to it.

Austen Leave them to what?

Hazel Oh, nothing. Nothing at all. Nothing.

Austen looks at her, then starts reading again, ignoring his sandwiches. There is silence for a moment

Austen Thirteen more shopping days to Christmas.

Rick comes back in, now dressed for bed — i.e. barefoot in pants and T-shirt. She lies on the bed under the duvet

The Lights come up on Warren's attic as the trap door opens and Warren emerges. He closes the trap door and bolts it

There is a peal of laughter from Marcie in the hall. Stanley puts his head round the door, still smiling

Stanley Hazel ...
Hazel Yes?
Stanley Marcie's off now, love. She's just off.
Hazel (*not moving*) Oh, right.

Marcie sticks her head round the door

Marcie Good-night, Mrs Inchbridge.
Hazel Good-night, Marcie.
Marcie Thank you for the tea.
Hazel My pleasure.
Marcie Good-night, Mr Skate.
Austen Good-night, Marcie.

Marcie goes

Hazel starts to eat Austen's sandwiches

Rick is still lying on the bed, staring

Pat's voice (*calling gently from the top of the stairs*) Alice! Alice! Come on, I know you're down there. Come on up now. He's gone out. Come on. Alice, don't be silly. Alice, he loves you really ...

Rick does not react

At the Inchbridges', Stanley returns to the sitting-room

Stanley What a nice kid that is.
Hazel (*munching*) Yes?
Stanley You should have stayed and talked to her, Hazel. She's a really nice, friendly girl.

Hazel Yes.

Stanley (*taking a sandwich as well*) Interested. In other people. That's quite rare these days. So many of them at that age, only interested in themselves. Sad.

Hazel Oh, yes.

Stanley I think you'd take to her, Hazel, if you gave her a chance.

Hazel (*rising suddenly*) I don't care what you do, Stanley, so long as you get it out of your system. And don't come crying to me when she's had enough of you, that's all.

She sweeps out

Stanley sits, stunned. He is aware of Austen

Austen (*smiling*) Don't mind me. Don't mind me.

Stanley goes out slowly

Austen hums a tune to himself for a second or so

We hear Thelma knocking on Warren's trap door

Thelma (*off*) Warren ... Warren ...

Warren (*irritably*) Yes?

Thelma (*off*) Do you want anything to eat, dear?

Warren No.

Thelma (*off*) Anything to drink? A little hot drink?

Warren No. No, thank you.

Thelma (*off*) Anything at all?

Warren (*shouting*) No, nothing. Nothing at all, Mother.

Silence

Thelma (*off*) I'll say a little prayer for you, son.

Warren sits on his bed in a state of extreme disquiet

There is a sudden knocking on Rick's basement door. Rick gets up at once, throwing aside the duvet. She turns on the light and moves to the door

Rick (*unlocking the door*) At last. What time do you call this, then ——?

Rick has barely unlocked the door when it is forced open from the other side and Larry, a powerful man in his mid-thirties, steps in, slams it shut, locks it and removes the key, which he pockets

(*Alarmed*) Who the hell are —— ?

Larry Where is she, then?

Rick (*outraged*) What do you think you're doing?

Larry Where is she? Come on, I know she's here. (*He moves into the room*) Marcie! Marcie!

Rick Look, what are you doing, there's nobody here.

Larry Don't tell me that. I've seen you both together. I saw you this evening, going out with her on your bike. Where is she?

Rick She's not here. There's nobody here. You get out. Before I call somebody.

Larry Christ, this place is a tip. What are you — squatting?

Rick No, I'm not. None of your business.

Larry (*looking further down the cellar*) Where's this lead?

Rick (*barring his way*) That is private property. Now get out. I tell you, she's not here.

Larry Listen, darling. I'm not stupid. (*He indicates the helmets*) Two little crash helmets, two little heads, all right? I can count. Now get out of my way.

Rick You go down there and I'll — I warn you ——

Larry makes to move further off down the cellar. Rick attempts a rather hasty, ill-aimed karate punch. Larry, with consummate ease, grabs both her wrists, pulls her to him and forces both arms up behind her back. Rick gasps with pain

Larry (*very quietly, his face an inch from Rick's*) You ever, ever try that again and I will break both your arms. All right?

Rick moans

(*Applying more pressure*) All right?

Rick (*reacting but refusing to scream: then, in a whisper*) Yes ...

Larry half carries Rick and seats her quite gently but firmly on the bed before releasing her. He pushes her gently back and lifts her feet so she is lying full out. Rick keeps her eyes fixed on him. She is literally frozen with fright. Larry picks the duvet off the floor and covers her with it. Just Rick's eyes peer out over the top of the cover

Larry (*softly, his face close to hers*) You lie there — absolutely still, do you hear? While I go and find my wife. (*He moves away, then turns suddenly*) Don't move. Or I will get cross. OK? Good girl.

*Larry goes off down into the cellar. Rick lies motionless, trying to follow
him with her eyes*

*Austen finishes reading the paper and crosses to the table. He sits before he
notices the empty plate*

Austen They've eaten all my sandwiches ...

Thelma knocks on Warren's trap door

*Under the next Austen disgustedly leaves the room, taking his plate and
newspaper with him. The Lights dim on the Inchbridges' sitting-room*

Thelma (*off*) Warren ... Warren, dear ...
Warren (*groaning*) Oh, Mother. What now?
Thelma (*off*) It's a woman to see you, Warren.
Warren (*alarmed*) A what?
Thelma (*off*)A young woman. A girl.
Warren Who? Who is it?
Marcie (*off*) It's me, Warren. It's Marcie.
Warren (*incredulously*) Marcie?
Marcie (*off*) Could I see you just for a second?
Warren (*bounding up*) Just a second. (*He attempts to tidy himself up and
open the trap door simultaneously*)
Marcie Hallo. May I come up?
Warren Yes. Yes, of course.

Marcie's head appears

Marcie (*calling down*) Thank you very much, Mrs Wrigley.
Thelma (*off*) Not at all. (*Anxiously*) Will you be all right, Warren?
Warren Yes, I'm fine, Mother. It's OK. It's OK. Don't worry.
Thelma (*off; doubtfully*) Yes.
Warren (*helping Marcie through*) Here ...
Marcie Thank you.

*Marcie arrives in the attic. She is carrying Warren's manuscript in its
envelope*

Thelma (*off*) Warren ...
Warren What is it, Mother ... ?
Thelma (*off*) You're not going to fall from grace, are you, son?

Marcie stares at Warren, slightly startled

Warren (*agonized*) Mother! (*He slams shut the trap door then realizes that Marcie is staring at him*) I'm sorry. It's just she ...

Marcie I know ——

Warren It's not that I ...

Marcie I understand.

Warren You do?

Marcie Absolutely.

Warren Ah!

Marcie I brought your manuscript. You left it at Mr Inchbridge's.

Warren Oh, thank you. Thanks very much. (*He offers her the chair*) Won't you ...?

Marcie Thank you. (*She sits*)

Warren sits on the bed. Marcie looks at him and smiles. Warren smiles weakly back. He is terrified. There is an awkward silence

At Rick's, Larry returns from the basement. Rick is still lying motionless, watching him

Larry (*looking up the stairs*) All right, she's up here then, is she? (*He makes to climb the stairs*)

Rick (*sitting up, alarmed*) No ...

Larry (*wheeling sharply*) Lie still!

Rick lies back immediately

(*Quieter*) Not a twitch. Not a whisper. All right? (*A fraction louder*) All right?

Rick (*in a whisper*) Right ...

Larry goes upstairs. Rick watches but doesn't move again

In the attic, Marcie breaks the silence at last

Marcie Isn't it amazing up here? What a room. (*She smiles*) I hope you don't mind. I read it. On my way here. Your statement.

Warren Oh.

Marcie Do you mind?

Warren No.

Marcie I just — sat in this bus shelter — waiting for this taxi — and I couldn't put it down. I only meant to look at the first page, really — but I got — I was going to return it tomorrow but once I'd read it I just had to — I mean, I didn't read it that carefully, I skimmed through a bit — but I think it's simply wonderful.

Warren You do?

Marcie Absolutely riveting. You must have the most brilliant, fantastic, imaginative, fertile brain I've ever met.

Warren Thank you.

Marcie I mean, your imagination is extraordinary. I knew it must be — from that game but — but this ...

Warren It's all true.

Marcie What?

Warren That — what I've written there. It's true.

Marcie True?

Warren Every word. I swear it. Promise.

Marcie (*breathlessly*) True? You mean, you're really ... You really believe you're ...

Warren I am.

Marcie (*in a whisper*) An alien?

Warren Yes.

Marcie (*quieter still*) Golly! (*She stares at him*) I'd like to read it again. Would you mind?

Warren No. Take it home.

Marcie No. Here, now. I have to read it now. (*She reads*)

During the following Warren falls asleep on the bed

Larry comes back down the stairs. Rick is lying under the duvet as before

Larry It is a stinking, disgusting sewer up there, isn't it? When did you last clean it? Eh? Revolting. Stomach-turning, that is. Some people. Animals. You're a little animal, aren't you? Like her. I thought women always prided themselves on being the clean ones. Revolting. (*He goes to the door*) Right. Here. (*He beckons her*)

Rick does not move

Come on. Come here. Or do you want me to come to you?

Rick gets out of bed and pads over to Larry

You give my wife a message. You tell her I called, that I'm sorry I missed her and that I will be back. You got that?

Rick nods

Good girl. (*He unlocks the door with the mortise key. He removes the key and holds it out*)

Rick makes to take the key

No, no. (*He indicates Rick's mouth*) Open. Come on, open wide.

Rick does so

(*Putting the key into Rick's mouth so that just the end sticks out*) I want this door left unlocked at all times. Understood? If I ever come back and find it locked, I will cause you to swallow that key. OK?

Rick nods

That's it. Back to bed, then.

Rick goes back to bed, the key still in her mouth

(*Switching off the light*) Sleep tight. Remember, I won't be far away.

Larry exits and closes the door

Rick allows herself a soft cry as she lies in the darkness

Stanley, now dressed for bed, comes into the sitting-room and stands in the darkened room by the window

Marcie finishes the manuscript. She looks up. Warren is snoring softly on the bed. Marcie smiles. Carefully, she lays down the script and tiptoes to the trap door, unbolts it and prepares to leave

Warren (*jolting awake; sleepily*) Marcie?
Marcie (*in a whisper*) Good-night, Warren.
Warren Did you ...?
Marcie Yes, I did.
Warren Did you ...?
Marcie It's so exciting, Warren, it has to be true.
Warren You're the only one who believes, you know, the only one.
Marcie I believe in you, Warren ...
Warren Marcie — it's just possible ... It's very possible that you could — you could be ...
Marcie An alien as well. The same as you?
Warren No, you're not a Lak, like me. Not from Lakkos but somewhere — I think — I'll have to check. I'll do some checking. I'll let you know ...
Marcie Yes, please. Do. Good-night. (*She starts to climb through the trap door*)

Warren Good-night, Marcie.

Marcie Warren ...

Warren What?

Marcie However much you feel you are, you're not alone, Warren. Never feel you're entirely alone ...

Marcie gives Warren a final smile and goes, closing the trap door behind her

Warren (*to himself, excitedly*) She is. She's one of us. She must be ... (*he lies back on the bed in great excitement but soon gets overtaken by sleep*)

The trap door slowly opens again

(*Sitting up excitedly. In a whisper*) Marcie?

A small portion of Thelma peeps through the half-open trap door

Thelma I prayed for you, son, I was praying for you ...

The trap door closes. Furious, Warren crosses and bolts it. The Lights fade on his attic

At the Inchbridges', Hazel, in her dressing gown, looks into the sitting-room and sees Stanley

Hazel Stanley, what are you doing?

Stanley Nothing, I was just ...

Hazel It's twenty-past three ...

Stanley Sorry.

Hazel Well, come to bed. I can't sleep when you're not in bed, you know that.

Stanley Sorry, I'll ... Sorry. (*He turns to follow her*)

Hazel There's no point in losing sleep dreaming about her, is there? If you want her, for God's sake have her, but have a little consideration for me as well.

Stanley Oh, Hazel ...

Hazel Come on. Upstairs.

Stanley You're going to drive me to it at this rate, you know, Hazel. You really are.

Hazel exits, followed by Stanley, saying the following as they go

Hazel Me? Oh, that's a new one, I must say ...

Stanley Hazel ...

They have both gone

> *There is a soft knocking on Rick's basement door. The handle is tried, the door is pushed open. Marcie cautiously puts her face around the door*

Marcie Rick ... Rick ... Rick, are you all right? Rick.

Rick moans from her bed.

> (*Hearing Rick*) Oh, dear God! (*She closes the door and crosses to the bed*) What's happened, Rick? What's happened, darling? (*She sits on the bed and clasps Rick to her*) What's the matter? Tell me?

Rick makes a gurgling sound

> What are you doing — with this ... What are you doing with this in your mouth? (*She pulls out the key*)

Rick gives a great sob

> Has he been here? Was this Larry? Did you let him in? Why the hell did you let him in?

Rick (*sobbing*) I — thought — it — was — you ...

Marcie What did he do? Did he hurt you?

Rick No ...

Marcie Then what ...?

Rick (*almost inaudible, her breath coming in great gasps*) I — was — just — so — frightened ...

Marcie What? What's that?

Rick Frightened. I — wanted — to — be — so — brave — for — you and — I was just — shit — scared ...

Marcie Shit scared? Yes. Well, I know how you feel. Why do you think I ran away from him?

Rick But — I wanted — to — be brave ...

Marcie (*soothing her*) Yes, OK. OK. And I need you to be brave, Rick. You see? I need you to be brave for me, my darling. Do you see? I need you. I need your courage. All right? Yes?

Rick (*recovering slightly*) Yes.

Marcie I need Herwin. I need my warrior to look after me. OK?

Rick Yes. (*She wriggles free of Marcie, climbs off the bed and marches to the door*)

Marcie (*slightly alarmed*) Where are you going?

Rick I'm going to lock this door. If he tries to get in again, I'll kill the bastard.

A swift cross-fade to the Inchbridges' sitting-room

> *Stanley enters in a much more positive mood than usual. He goes to the sideboard and, taking out the game, starts to lay it out on the table as before. He calls out as he does this*

Stanley All right, all right, everyone. If we're all here we ought to get started. We've got a lot to get through this evening. There are battles to be fought and won ... come on in. Come through. (*He finds he has a figure missing*) That's odd ... Where's Idonia?

> *Hazel enters with the anglepoise. She seems to have sharpened her image slightly. Maybe it's the new dress. She has a "new-look" Idonia figure in her hand, but well hidden*

Hazel. I've lost Idonia. Have you seen her?

Hazel Oh, yes. I—I've re-dressed her.

Stanley Re-dressed? How do you mean?

Hazel (*fixing the lamp to the table*) I felt she needed a change of image.

Stanley Really? I thought she looked fine. Where is she?

> *Warren comes in with a couple of chairs and Rick with a third. They place these around the table*

The whole group has an excitement, a tension about it

Right. Quick as we can, well done. We must get started. Sit down, everyone.

They all sit

Got the parameters, Warren?

Warren Yes. But we know where we're going.

Stanley Yes. This time to Balaac. Where's Marcie?

Rick She was in the bathroom. She's just coming.

Stanley Do the lights for us, Warren, will you?

Warren Yes, Mr Inchbridge ... (*He starts to rise*)

> *Marcie enters. She has a small game figure with her*

Marcie I'll do it. (*She switches off the overhead lights. She appears more excited than any of them*) Sorry. Off we go then. Hallo, Warren.

Warren Hallo. (*He hastily whispers to Marcie*) I think I've got some great news for you ...

Marcie (*whispering back*) What?

Stanley Oh, we need the salt-cellar again. (*To Hazel*) We need Marcie's salt-cellar, dear.

Marcie No, that's OK. There! (*She puts the small figure she has been holding down on the board. Her figure is attractive, a little like a character from "Flash Gordon" or a more exotic episode of "Star Trek"*) Brought my own this week.

Stanley Oh, that's lovely.

Warren Terrific.

Rick Great.

Stanley Isn't that beautiful, Hazel?

Hazel Yes. There! (*She puts down her new "Idonia" figure next to Marcie's. Hazel's tends to the romantic, even younger than before—a long frock and flowing hair. There is a definite contest in prospect*)

Stanley Good heavens, just look at that.

Warren Ah.

Marcie How lovely. Simply lovely. Congratulations. Did you make it yourself, Hazel?

Hazel (*smugly*) Yes, I did.

Marcie I wish I was that clever with my hands.

Hazel I expect you can be when you need to be.

Marcie looks rather puzzled

Stanley Right, everyone. Concentration. We must now set out on what might well be our final journey of the game. To death or victory.

Warren Death or victory!

All Death or victory!

Stanley To the south, then ... Onward ...

They move their pieces, one by one, across the board, step by step

Are you ready and armed, Herwin?

Rick Ready and armed, Wise One.

Stanley What do you sense, Idonia child ... ?

Hazel Hurdle-murre-durne ... I sense great danger, Wise One ...

Stanley What do you see and hear, Xenon, the Stranger?

Warren I hear Balaac. I do not yet see him. He is distant but approaching slowly.

Stanley Good. Onward!

Hazel Onward!

Warren Onward!

Rick Onward!
Marcie (*excitedly*) Onward!
Stanley What can you report now?
Hazel Troodle-smaire-hart ... The danger increases still more, Wise One.
  Clouds are gathering. There is impenetrable darkness ahead.
Warren Balaac has sensed our presence. He is starting to approach more
  rapidly. I cannot yet see him.

The sound of wind can be faintly heard now

Stanley Onward!
Hazel Onward!
Rick Onward!
Marcie (*goading them on*) Onward!
Hazel Broochj! Broochj! There is a wind. A terrible storm approaching. And
  with it comes deep, deep evil.
Warren Balaac is approaching very fast now. He is riding the very wind
  itself ...

Under the next the wind effect builds to a crescendo

Stanley Onward!
Hazel Onward!
Rick Onward!
Marcie (*almost screaming with excitement*) Onward!
Hazel Oorspickle-gerdiff .... He rides with the storm. The lightning is his
  bridle and his hoofs are the thunder ...
Warren He's very close, very close now, but I still can't see him ... Where
  is he? Where is he? Why can't I see him?

They are all now having to shout over the wind

Stanley Ready, Herwin?
Rick Ready. I'm ready ... Let him come ...

There begins now a growing thunderous roar, building to a wail

Warren He's here, he's here ... He's here amongst us ... Why can't we see
  him ...?
Hazel Oh, my God, what's happening, what's happening ...?
Stanley Stay calm, everybody ...

Rick gives a great war-like yell, stands and raises her arms above her head.

Marcie yells. Hazel screams. There is a sudden, final thunderous explosion as if the devil's hoofbeats had ridden over them. Rick sits. Silence

Hazel (*after a moment, nervously, in a small voice — half Idonia's, half her own*) What's happening to us? What's happening? Stanley?
Warren Wise One?
Stanley   ... Er ... I'm ... I'm ...

They are all looking at him, expectantly

(*Pulling himself together*) ... Er ... fear not, friends. (*More confidently*) Fear not. (*With sudden authority*) Fear not!
Marcie (*her face radiant from the experience*) Fantastic!

Black-out

ACT II

The same. A few days later

In the basement, Rick is preparing a meal. It is hardly a banquet but at least it's an effort. Marcie's influence is here seen at work. The room, too, has taken on a generally tidier appearance. We will see Rick from time to time during the next

We will also see Warren, who is busily installing a great deal more wiring. This entails him appearing and disappearing through his trap door at odd intervals as he pays out cable from a drum. The cables in turn are connected via a mixer to his computer system

At the Inchbridges', Stanley enters breathlessly. He carries a small package. He is cheerful and positive. He is followed by Marcie, who is laughing. They both slump in chairs, exhausted

Stanley What on earth have you bought? What have you been buying, woman?

Marcie (*excitedly*) Oh, everything. Don't ask. Everything. Lucky I met you, wasn't it? I can't even remember half the things now. I bought the shop. I'm hopeless. I just see things, I want them, I can't afford them but I buy them. I just love Christmas, don't you? I love giving presents. My whole family are like that. We all used to give each other ten presents each. When I was a kid on Christmas morning you could barely see the Christmas tree. Just this mountain of wrapping paper.

Stanley Do you have a large family?

Marcie Two sisters, a brother. My mother, father. Uncles and aunts and cousins and things. Quite big.

Stanley Will you be going home for Christmas?

Marcie (*frowning slightly*) No. Not this year.

In the basement, Rick comes on to lay the table: two bowls, two spoons, new salt and pepper mills

(*After a slight pause*) We — my father doesn't — isn't talking to me. He didn't approve of my marriage.

Stanley I thought you said that was over.

Marcie It is.

Stanley Well?
Marcie No. They wouldn't approve of that either. It's difficult. They're —
very conventional people.
Stanley Ah.

Rick goes off again

What do they do?
Marcie My father's an MP.
Stanley (*impressed*) Is he?
Marcie Not a very important one.
Stanley Oh.
Marcie So's my mother.
Stanley An MP?
Marcie Yes. She's slightly more important. She's a shadow something. I
forget.
Stanley Oh. And do they ——?
Marcie (*restlessly*) I don't think I want to talk about me any more, do you
mind?
Stanley No, of course. I'm sorry. I was just ...

Marcie rises and paces about

*Warren appears in his attic and in due course disappears, busy with his
wiring*

Marcie Will my stuff be all right in the hall there?
Stanley Yes, sure. Hazel must still be out. And Austen won't be back for a
little bit. Sit down.
Marcie I'll go in a minute. When I've got my breath back.
Stanley How will you get home with all that?
Marcie I can get a taxi from the corner. (*She looks around*) I haven't been
here since — since the night we played the game.
Stanley Not that long ago. Less than a week.
Marcie Wasn't it extraordinary? It couldn't really have been a freak storm,
could it? I know that's what we all agreed it had to be — but it must have
been more than that. What do you think it was?
Stanley (*the schoolteacher*) I think it might — well — I believe it could have
been an accumulation — a sort of freak gathering of a great deal of psychic
energy. I think as a group we must have been given off an abnormal
amount. For some reason. And maybe — like a capacitor — an electrical
capacitor does — our combined energies reached a level where they
simply discharged ... I mean, that's just a theory.
Marcie It sounds a good one to me ...

Stanley I don't think you'd get many scientists to believe it.

Marcie (*dismissively*) Scientists? What do they know? I'd sooner listen to someone like you. Someone who relates things to people, even if they're wrong.

Stanley (*doubtfully*) Well, thank you.

Marcie I bet you're a marvellous teacher.

Stanley Well ...

Marcie I wish you'd taught me. My teachers were all — awful. Dull. Dead. I don't think any of them had been outside the school building since nineteen-fifty.

Stanley Where were you educated?

Marcie (*evasive again*) Oh, you wouldn't know it — let's not talk about me, please. I hate it.

Stanley Why not? I'm interested.

Marcie In me?

Stanley Yes.

Marcie I'm not very interesting.

Stanley You're very interesting.

Marcie Am I?

Stanley Very. I want to know all about you.

Marcie Perhaps. One day. Not now.

Rick returns, stirring a saucepan of thick soup. She tastes it, wrinkles her nose and adds salt from the salt-mill

Will you carry on playing the game?

Stanley Probably. (*Only half joking*) If you'll promise to come, that is.

Marcie I don't think I should, you know. Seriously.

Stanley Why not?

Marcie I'm not one of the group, am I? Not really.

Stanley You are.

Marcie I don't think some of you feel I am.

Stanley Who?

Marcie Well — Hazel, really.

Stanley Ah.

Marcie I don't know why she doesn't like me but she doesn't. I can't think what I'm supposed to have done, can you?

Stanley (*a little guiltily*) No.

Marcie Well, can you? I can't think what. Sometimes I just seem to do that to people.

Stanley You've done nothing.

Marcie It's a pity. I like her. I think we could have been really, really friendly. Still ... Maybe she's more of a man's woman. Do you think that's it?

Stanley (*doubtfully*) No. I wouldn't have described her as that.

Marcie It must be me, then. Never mind. It happens. There was a girl at school like that. But I found out later it was because I stole her best friend.
Stanley Ah.
Marcie Did you have a best friend?
Stanley At school?
Marcie Yes.
Stanley Yes, I think so. It was — rather a long time ago.
Marcie I had hundreds. I love having friends.

Hazel comes in. She is in her coat and has obviously just arrived home. She has had her hair done. She looks a lot younger. Her manner, too, is bright and chirpy — if a little brittle

Hazel (*entering*) ... what on earth is all that stuff in the hall? Who's been ... (*She sees them both*) Whoops! Sorry, beg your pardon!

She goes out again along the hall

(*Off*) Sorry! Sorry!
Stanley (*vainly*) Hazel!
Hazel (*off; distant*) Sorry!
Stanley (*embarrassed, to Marcie*) Sorry.
Marcie She's had her hair done differently.
Stanley Yes. Has she?
Marcie Suits her. It's much nicer.
Stanley I'll — tell her.
Marcie You should. Women like to be told. It shows you've noticed them.
Stanley Yes.

A pause

Warren reappears again with more wire. He disappears in due course

Your hair's nice, I always think.
Marcie *My* hair?
Stanley Yes.
Marcie My hair's horrible. I loathe my hair. If we're going to start discussing my hair, I'm off. (*She rises again*)

Stanley rises too

Austen enters with the evening paper

Austen (*entering*) ... what's all this —— (*He sees them*) Ah! Good-evening.

Good-evening, Marcie.

Marcie Evening, Mr Skate.

Austen Is that your accumulation of purchases out there on the floor, is it?

Marcie Yes, I'm sorry.

Austen I nearly had occasion to fall over them, did you know that?

Marcie I'm very sorry.

Austen Never, young lady, on any account leave obstructions in a passage-way. It's very dangerous. You should know that.

Stanley She's just off ...

Austen Are you cognizant with the percentage of accidents that occur in the home?

Marcie No. Lots, I imagine.

Austen Would you care to hazard a guess?

Stanley Austen, Marcie's going now ...

Austen Well, may I suggest that the next time, young lady, the next time you contemplate depositing a positive pile, a huge hummock, a massive mountain, a considerable cumulus of stuff about the place, you stop and spare a thought for other people. Enough said?

Marcie (*chastened*) Sorry, Mr Skate.

Stanley Tumulus.

Austen Eh?

Stanley Tumulus. You said cumulus. I think you meant tumulus. Tumulus is a mound, originally a burial mound. Whereas cumulus is a rain cloud. Sorry to correct you, Austen, but I know how punctilious you are about those sort of things.

Austen stares at him in amazement

You know that word, punctilious? It means precise observation to detail; exact attention to form; nit-picking.

Stanley and Marcie go out. During the following, Stanley wanders back into the sitting-room

Austen sits slowly

Rick returns with the pan again. She tastes the soup with disapproval and decides to grind in some pepper

Warren returns to his room and sits at the console. He switches on his screen. A beeping sound is heard

Warren (*muttering*) Great. Great. Gotcha. (*He sets to work, connecting the wires he has run to the console*)

Stanley picks up his package and moves to exit

Hazel bounces in

Hazel (*brightly*) Oh — has she gone? What a pity, I was going to make us all some tea. Never mind. She'll be popping in again before long, I expect. Won't she?

Hazel goes out again, singing loudly with more volume than tune. We hear her in the kitchen, crashing about

Stanley stares after her rather despairingly. Austen looks at Stanley over the top of his newspaper. Stanley sees Austen looking at him and shrugs rather ineffectually. This seems to be the final straw as far as Austen's concerned. He folds up the paper and lays it down

Stanley heads for the exit

Austen (*sharply*) Just a minute!
Stanley (*startled*) What?
Austen (*rising*) Just a minute. Just a minute. (*He pauses*) Just a minute. (*He gathers his thoughts*)

Stanley waits. Hazel sings on in the kitchen

I presume you are aware that you are driving my sister to the brink of a nervous breakdown? Are you aware of that fact?
Stanley Rubbish.
Austen It's a fact. Listen.

They listen. Hazel sings, stopping during the following

Correct me if I'm wrong, but isn't that the sound of a woman losing her reason?
Stanley It's the sound of a woman singing.
Austen (*shouting angrily*) No, it isn't. Not any woman. That is the sound of *Hazel* singing. My sister. Hazel never used to sing like that. Hazel never used to sing at all. All through our childhood I never remember her singing. Hazel is tone-deaf. Like all our family. I am telling you for a fact, Inchbridge, that is the sound of a woman in mental torment. That is the sound of a woman driven to desperation by a husband flaunting his whores and peccadilloes right under his own wife's nose in her own front room.
Stanley How dare you?

Austen Don't interrupt me. I am warning you, Inchbridge, if my sister loses one iota of her mental stability because of your moral misdemeanours, I will have you in court, so help me I will.

Stanley In court? On what grounds?

Austen (*beside himself with fury*) On the grounds that you are a bastard, that's why. A lecherous, insensitive, died-in-the-wool bastard! Have you anything to say for yourself, anything?

Stanley (*looking at him for a second*) Oh, get stuffed, Austen. If anyone's driven her barmy, it's you. You've driven us both round the bend. You saw your own wife off and then started on us.

Austen How dare you insinuate that about my wife. Mary died in considerable pain ...

Stanley Mary died with indecent haste. She couldn't wait to get shot of you, poor cow ...

Austen You will retract that statement immediately.

Stanley You got shot of her and then you started on us. And, by God, you've succeeded. You've hounded us, Austen. You've hovered over our marriage like some bloody great stuffed albatross.

Austen I'm noting all this down, Inchbridge, never fear.

Stanley Hazel and I have never had a moment to ourselves since the day we were married. We could never even make love properly because you were listening at the door ...

Austen That's a lie, I never stooped to that ——

Stanley We could hear you, Austen, we heard you stooping and breathing and wheezing through our bedroom keyhole. We could never be properly alone anywhere. Not in the house. Anywhere. You even sat behind us in the cinema ...

Austen That was pure coincidence and you know it ...

Stanley What, in Norwich? That was supposedly our honeymoon, Austen. Two weeks on the Broads and you waiting at every bloody lock with a movie camera ——

Austen All right, so I cared about Hazel. I worried for her. I'm not ashamed of that ...

Stanley (*ploughing on*) — every time we tried to talk to each other you sat there correcting our grammar — you've had us waiting on you hand and foot for fifteen years and we've never had one word of thanks. You've treated me like a lodger and Hazel like a housekeeper. Anything that's happened in this house is entirely due to you, Austen ... You're the reason that's going on out there ...

Austen Oh, no, the reason for that ... I'll tell you in one word the reason for that. Betrayal. You have betrayed my sister, Inchbridge.

Stanley Oh, don't be so bloody melodramatic ...

Austen You've thrown her over for some passing piece of skirt half your age and left her with nothing. You weren't man enough even to give Hazel children.

Stanley (*low*) I rather left that to you, Austen. I thought you considered that your job.

Silence. Even Hazel has stopped singing

Austen (*quietly*) Get out. Get out of this house. (*He appears to be having trouble breathing*) Do you hear me? I want you out. Out, now. You will not make allegations of that nature and stay under my roof.

Stanley OK. Fine. OK.

Austen You haven't heard the end of this. Oh, no. No. I have ways. Don't worry. I have ways. Make no mistake, we haven't yet finished with this little matter, you and me.

Stanley I.

Austen What?

Stanley You and I. You said you and me. You and I.

Austen opens and shuts his mouth and looks as if he might explode

Austen I'm going upstairs to my room. By the time I come down, I want you out of this house, all right?

Stanley Suits me.

Austen goes out. He looks distinctly shaky

Stanley stands and watches him

Rick returns with her saucepan and tries more salt in the soup

Warren labours on in his attic. He appears to be nearing completion

Hazel comes in with a jam-jar full of flowers. She puts them on the table and stands back to admire them

Hazel There. Don't they look pretty?

Stanley Yes. Hazel, those are dandelions.

Hazel I know. I picked them for your little friend. I thought they might make her wet the bed. (*She giggles*) Doodle-addle-doodle-oodle ...

She goes out

Stanley (*appalled*) Oh, my God. What have I done?

*At Warren's, because the trap door is open, we hear the front doorbell ring.
Warren stops what he is doing and turns up his computer screen volume. The
beeping sound, as before. Warren studies the screen intently. The beeping
gets more rapid*

Then we hear Thelma's voice from the bottom of the ladder

Thelma (*off*) Warren, Warren, dear ...

Warren turns down his volume

Stanley exits during the next

Warren What is it, Mother?
Thelma (*off*) There's that young woman here again, Warren ...
Warren Well, show her up, Mother, show her up.
Thelma (*off*) She's come in a taxi, Warren.
Warren Yes, all right.
Thelma (*off, filled with foreboding*) Oh, son. I hope you're allowing the Lord
  to guide your footsteps.
Warren Every inch of the way, Mother. Will you let her in?
Thelma (*off*) You are going to tidy all this wire up soon, aren't you, dear?
Warren Yes, Mother. Don't touch anything.
Thelma (*off, her voice receding*) Only someone's going to trip over it ...

*Warren turns up the volume and studies the screen for a second. There are
now double beeps*

Marcie (*off*) Warren, it's me. Marcie. May I come up?
Warren (*turning down the screen again*) Yes, sure.

Marcie's head appears through the trap door. She is carrying a book

Marcie What on earth are you doing? The house is full of wires. It's like a
  snake-pit. I brought back your book. (*She climbs up*) What's going on? Are
  you building something special?

Warren helps Marcie through the trap door

  Thanks.
Warren (*secretively*) It's nothing. Just security.
Marcie Security?
Warren (*closing the trap door*) What did you make of the book?

Marcie Oh, Mr Van der Hooch. Fantastic.

Warren But true, though.

Marcie Well ...

Warren He spent twenty years of his life on that, you know.

Marcie Yes, I read.

Warren He wouldn't have given up a university career like he had for nothing, would he ...?

Marcie Yes, but I thought they ——

Warren What?

Marcie I thought they — sort of sacked him ...

Warren And did you read why?

Marcie ... Er ... for falsifying results, wasn't it?

Warren No, no, no. Wrong.

Marcie Ah. I thought ...

Warren For arriving at results that threw all other accepted conventionally held theories out of the window. Not just the laws of physics, but chemistry, astronomy, biology, even gravity ...

Marcie Yes, I see.

Warren Electromagnetics, relativity. Arnie stood them all on their head. And for that they hounded him ...

Marcie Yes.

Warren He lived in a hut on nothing but raw reindeer meat for twenty years, you know ...

Marcie That doesn't sound too good. (*She pauses slightly*) Is your mother all right? She looks a bit ——

Warren Oh, she'll be fine. It's just that we are going through a critical phase at present. She and I.

Marcie How do you mean?

Warren Well, as I told you, she is an Orgue. They are a hardy species, very loyal but of limited intelligence. They are used on Lakkos — which is where I am originally from, of course — I am a Lak ——

Marcie Yes, I know ...

Warren — the Laks, being of a higher intelligence, use the Orgues to mind their children until the young Lak reaches maturity. At this point in the relationship, the Orgue ceases to be important and the Lak becomes naturally dominant.

Marcie Yes, I see. Complicated. What happens to the poor old Orgue?

Warren Ah well. They are either discarded or occasionally they're kept as pets.

Marcie Well, I hope maybe you'll hang on to your mother.

Warren Possibly. We'll see. We'll see.

Marcie (*gently*) When is it you — when do you expect to reach this maturity, then, Warren?

Warren Any day now I will undergo a change — during which I must keep my mother away and then, *voilà*.

Marcie Will you — look any different?

Warren Not — to the naked eye. But ... to certain people, yes.

Marcie Who? Like who?

Warren (*deciding this is the moment*) Well, this is the news I wanted to tell you. I think, Marcie, that you're almost certainly a Trilla.

Marcie A Trilla? Me? What's a Trilla?

Warren T-R-I-double L-A.

Marcie How pretty.

Warren They are. They're some of the most beautiful beings in the universe. In your natural state you'd be even more incredibly beautiful than you are now.

Marcie My natural state?

Warren Stripped of your human characteristics.

Marcie Oh, I see.

Warren The point is — this is the exciting bit — the Trillas and the Laks were once one being. They had a symbiotic relationship. But they were split apart at the crash.

Marcie I see. I see.

Warren But once in a while, by chance, both halves get reunited and together they become the most beautiful and powerful creature in the universe. Arnie told of a dream he once had, long ago, in which a Trilla visited him. And she floated at the foot of his bed and divested herself of her coverings till she was naked for him. And Arnie said it was at that moment that he experienced that deep pain that could only be sensed through the deepest pleasure.

Marcie Ah.

Warren Now it's very possible that once I've — you know — changed — we might both recognize that beauty in each other ... (*He moves closer to Marcie*)

Marcie (*rising*) Yes. I've got this taxi waiting at the moment, Warren, so I won't ...

Warren That's my hope. That would make us together something wonderful.

Marcie Well, we'll see. Sorry, I ——

Warren Yes. Right. See you Thursday ...

Marcie — er ... yes. Sure. Bye.

Marcie starts to climb down the ladder again

Under the next, Hazel comes into her sitting-room with her needlework basket and sits at the table. She begins working intently on something very small. She is immensely concentrated on this, like a child

Warren Bye.
Marcie Warren?
Warren Um?
Marcie Be as nice as you can to your mother, won't you?
Warren Oh, sure.

Marcie goes

Warren closes the trap door and goes quickly back to his screen. We hear the double beeps as before

She's beautiful, Arnie. You're right. She's sheer, total beauty.

In a moment, Warren sets to work again on his wiring

Rick puts more salt in her soup and goes off again

Stanley comes on rather anxiously

Stanley (*calling*) Hazel ... Hazel ... (*He stops as he sees Hazel at work at the table*)
Hazel (*without looking up*) Mmm.
Stanley Do we — do we have Dr Blake's phone number anywhere?
Hazel (*still absorbed*) It's in my address book.
Stanley Right. (*He looks around*) And where's your address book?
Hazel In the kitchen.
Stanley It's just that — well, I was passing Austen's room and I heard him ... He's lying on his bed, he's a very strange colour — and I think he's having trouble breathing ... I think it could be a stroke — or a fit — or a heart attack ...
Hazel (*still concentrating*) Oh dear ...
Stanley So I think we'd better — hadn't we? Yes. Hazel, what are you doing?
Hazel (*still not looking up*) I'm making something for me ...
Stanley What are you making?
Hazel A little dress. (*She holds up a tiny frock for a small child figure*) Look ...
Stanley Ah, yes. Lovely. (*He laughs nervously*) A bit — small, isn't it?
Hazel (*scornfully*) It's not for me, you silly. It's for Idonia. For little Idonia.
Stanley (*greatly relieved*) Oh, for little Idonia. Oh, splendid! Look, I'm going to phone Blake ... Are you going to — look in on Austen, are you?
Hazel (*returning to her work*) When I've finished this.
Stanley (*staring at Hazel*) Yes. Right.

Stanley goes out, leaving Hazel still concentrating on her task

During the next Hazel finishes and leaves the room, taking her work basket

There is a knocking on the basement door

Rick hurries on and is about to open the door but checks herself in time

Rick (*calling*) Who is it?
Marcie (*off*) Marcie. It's Marcie. Sorry I'm late.
Rick (*unlocking the door*) About time ... (*She opens the door*)

Marcie staggers in with a couple of large carrier bags

Marcie (*breathlessly*) Sorry, I was ... (*She calls to someone behind her*) Thanks very much.
Rick Who's that?
Marcie Taxi driver. He was a terribly nice man. He's got a son at Keele University ...

Marcie dumps down the bags and returns outside for more packages

Rick You're still taking taxis ...
Marcie I had to. Look at it all. Look at what I've got. Give us a hand.

During the following, Rick and Marcie carry in more parcels. Marcie's shopping spree extends to six carriers similar in size to the first two and a couple of big square parcels

Rick (*carrying things in*) What have you bought here?
Marcie (*secretively*) Ha-ha! You'll have to wait till next week, won't you? Wait till Christmas.

Rick closes and locks the door

Marcie takes off her coat and goes off briefly to hang it up

Rick (*surveying the parcels*) How much have you spent? (*To herself*) How much has she spent?
Marcie (*off*) Mmm! What's the delicious smell? Hey! You've christened the stove!

She enters

Did it work all right?

Rick Yes. Just plugged it in.

Marcie Brilliant. Glad one of us is technically minded. What are you cooking?

Rick Oh, some — soup. Sort of soup. Want to try it?

Marcie (*tidying away some of her packages*) You bet. Sort of soup is just the sort of thing I could do with.

Rick exits

Rick (*as she goes*) I don't know what it'll be like.

Marcie I haven't eaten all day. (*During the following, she surveys the table a trifle critically and rearranges Rick's primitive setting a little*) Sorry I'm late. I stopped off to see Warren. He's — well, I think he's some sort of genius. He has to be. He's just — not of this world, is he?

Rick returns with the saucepan

Rick He's mad. (*She moves to put the pan straight on to the table*)

Marcie (*stopping Rick*) Hang on, don't burn the table ...

Rick Doesn't matter, does it?

Marcie (*slipping a magazine under the pan*) Well, silly to do that. Now, what have we here? Smells wonderful. You know, I'm starving, I haven't eaten since this morning.

Rick serves up

(*Sitting*) What we need is a tureen. Or a bowl, don't we? Yum. Do with some mats, too.

Rick hands Marcie a bowl of soup

Thank you. It's home-made, isn't it? And proper soup spoons, I suppose. Eventually.

Rick (*sitting*) Right. Cheers.

Marcie Cheers!

There is silence while they both take a mouthful or two. It's obviously revolting but Marcie puts a brave face on it

Golly! It's wonderful. Really unusual. Is this the first time you've made it?

Rick (*her eyes watering from the taste*) Yes.

Marcie How clever. Did you use a recipe?

Rick (*choking*) No.

During the following, Rick takes both their bowls, tips them back into the saucepan and takes both that and the bowls back into the kitchen area; then she returns and sits

Marcie Well, I think that's brilliant. I could never do that. There are some people who are just natural instinctive cooks. Give them a stove and a handful of ingredients and they can just concoct something out of thin ... (*She tails away*)

There is a silence

I wasn't really that hungry.

There is a silence

You can't blame yourself if you don't get it absolutely perfectly right first time. It's very, very difficult ...

Rick (*bitterly*) Unless you're an instinctive cook ...

Marcie Well. Neither am I. You can't cook anything properly, anyway, on that thing. We need a proper stove.

Rick looks miserable

I'll make us some coffee.

Marcie exits, leaving Rick alone

Warren, in his attic, appears to have completed another phase in his wiring programme. He opens the trap door. He has a microphone on his console with a switch, which he now presses down. His voice booms round the house downstairs

Warren This is Warren Wrigley testing — one — two — three — four ...

There is a distant cry of alarm from Thelma

(*Contentedly, to himself*) Good. Good.

Thelma (*off*) Warren ... Warren ...

Warren What is it, Mother?

Thelma (*off*) What's happening, Warren?

Warren Nothing to worry about, Mother. I was just testing. You go back to bed.

Thelma (*off*) How did you know I was in bed?

Warren I know where you are at all times, Mother, remember that. Now go to bed.

Thelma (*off, departing*) I thought it was your father. Returned to us.

Warren closes the trap door, irritated by this interruption. He studies his master wiring diagram. Under the next, he opens the trap door again and climbs down, clutching the diagram and frowning

Marcie returns with two mugs of coffee

Marcie I couldn't see any milk, I don't know if you remembered to ——
Rick No, I forgot.
Marcie Oh, it doesn't matter. Better for us, anyway. (*She puts one mug down by Rick and sits apart from her*) Actually, let's face it, what we need is a fridge, don't we? We need a lot of things really. (*She pauses*) I—I might as well tell you. While you were out yesterday, I had a look upstairs ...

Rick looks at her sharply

I'm sorry. I know you never want anyone to go up there but — well, it's such a waste, isn't it? It's vast. There's those three bedrooms and that huge sitting-room and a lovely big bathroom. And the kitchen's huge. It's a lovely room. It could be. It's such a waste. Don't you think so, really?

Rick does not reply

I mean, I know it would need masses doing to it, but ... We could really make it wonderful. Between us. It needn't cost a lot. It's all there. Basically.

Silence

I'm sorry. Are you very angry with me? Why can't you go up there? Is it — because of them? Your parents? Well, your mother and ... But, Rick, darling, they've gone, haven't they? They're not there now. Are they part of the dreams you have? You do know you dream, don't you? Shout out in the night. You're always doing it. (*She laughs*) I thought the house was on fire the first night you ...

There is a pause

Actually, I must tell you — I had this awful fear that you'd ... that they were — your parents were up there murdered or something. In a cupboard. You'd done them to death. There was this awful smell. But that just turned out to be the food. There was still this meal laid out — well, the remains of it — on the kitchen table. Was that the meal she left

for you the day they ...? Yes. Must have been. God! (*She shivers*) Yes,
I did, I read the note as well. I'm sorry. I told you I'm a terribly nosy
person. I didn't realize. Is that your real name? Alice? Alice. It's a lovely
name.

There is still no response from Rick

(*Suddenly standing*) Listen. Will you do something for me? For me? Will
you? Come upstairs with me. Now.

Rick looks at her again.

(*Holding out her hand*) Come on. Please. For me. Please. There's nothing
there to be frightened of. No-one. Trust me. (*She takes Rick's hand*)

Rick allows herself to be led to the foot of the stairs

Come on. That's it. I'll be with you, darling. Come on, Rick. Alice? Are
you ready? OK?
Rick (*dully*) On one condition.
Marcie (*gently*) What's that?
Rick Never ever, ever call me Alice ...
Marcie I promise.

They climb the stairs slowly together

*The Lights fade on the attic and basement and concentrate on the Inchbridges'
sitting-room. From somewhere along the hall comes the sound of a Christmas carol recording*

> *Stanley hurries in with a tray plus a bottle of sherry and four glasses,
> speaking as he enters. He places the tray on the sideboard and starts to
> pour out drinks during the next. He is followed by Warren with the
> anglepoise, which he, in turn, attaches to the table, plugs in, and switches
> on. Both men are extremely positive in manner. Indeed, the whole house
> tonight is filled with confidence and goodwill*

Stanley (*entering*) ... might as well push the boat out a bit seeing as it's
Christmas, eh?
Warren Very nice idea, Mr Inchbridge.
Stanley Warren, I really ... Hazel and I really appreciate your coming round
tonight — of all nights ...
Warren That's all right, Mr Inchbridge ...

Stanley No, I mean. Christmas Eve — you and Rick, you both would probably have preferred to spend it with your nearest and dearest. Sherry?
Warren Thank you very much.
Stanley Well, I don't think we need wait for them. Good health. Happy Christmas.
Warren Happy Christmas, Mr Inchbridge.

They drink

Stanley Mmm. Not bad. Not too bad.
Warren Very nice.
Stanley Yes. Smooth. It has a good nose. (*He tastes the sherry again*) Mellow. Palatable. Mmmm. Mmmm?
Warren (*tasting again*) Mmmm. Mmmm.
Stanley (*agreeing with him*) Mmmm. How's your mother? Coping with Christmas, is she?
Warren Oh, yes, she's under control.
Stanley Good.

Rick comes in with two kitchen chairs. She, too, is bright and — for her — positive

Ah, Rick. A glass of sherry?
Rick Thank you very much, Mr Inchbridge.
Stanley Coming up. Warren and I think it's quite a good one. We'd like your opinion. (*He pours another glass*)

Rick sets the chairs round the table

I don't know if Hazel will want one. Warren, would you mind — just asking my wife if she'd like a glass?
Warren Certainly, Mr Inchbridge.

Warren exits

Stanley Where is she? I presume she intends to join us?
Rick She was just putting things out in the kitchen. (*She takes the glass*) Thank you.
Stanley Good health. Yes. Hazel's made us a little snack. For afterwards. When we've finished playing.

Warren enters

Warren She says no, thank you, she's having a fruit juice.

Stanley Oh, well. More for us, eh?

Warren She's made this big orange jelly.

Stanley Has she? Splendid. (*During the next, he gets out the game board and the box of figures*)

Warren And a lot of blancmange.

Stanley Yes, well. She always could make a fine blancmange, could Hazel.

Rick Is it meant for us?

Stanley Yes. Yes, I think it probably is. Yes.

Warren (*enthusiastically*) Great.

Rick (*less sure*) Yes.

There is a pause

Stanley (*casually, as he sets out the board*) So, what's all your news, Rick? How's Marcie? Is she well?

Rick She's fine.

Stanley Good. I haven't seen her for a day or so. Give her my love, won't you?

Rick Sure.

Stanley (*after a slight pause*) You will remember, won't you?

Rick Yes.

There is a pause. Along the hall, the music is switched off. Hazel's voice takes up the singing

Warren How's Mr Skate, Mr Inchbridge? Is he any better?

Stanley They're keeping him in a day or two longer, Warren — thank you for asking. Giving him one or two more tests. They're pretty certain it was a mild stroke. Just a warning.

Warren Ah.

Hazel enters. Her reversion to more youthful days continues. She has on a very short skirt, bright tights and has redone her hair in an even younger style. The effect is incongruous but not grotesque. She has a tall glass of fruit squash, which she is drinking through a straw. She's especially bouncy

Hazel Sorry, folks ... Here I am. Let's get going, I'm ready. (*She sits*)

Stanley (*slightly startled*) Right. Good, well, yes, let's start. (*He indicates the lights*) Warren, would you mind ...

Warren switches off the lights. The rest of them sit around the table

Let's see what perils lie in wait for our intrepid band this evening, eh?

Hazel "gurgles" with her straw as she sucks on her drink

So long as we don't have a repetition of last week.

Hazel No way.

Stanley Sorry?

Hazel That won't happen again.

Stanley What makes you so sure?

Hazel We're the right number. Last week we had the wrong cosmic number ...

Stanley (*doubtful*) Yes, I suppose ...

Warren That's possible.

Hazel It's true, dreep-droop-dee-doop-bee-barp! Brerrp! Idonia, the Mystic, has spoken.

Rick (*removing the figure of Idonia from the box and staring at it*) Hey! What's happened to Idonia? What have you done to her?

Hazel I just made her some new clothes ...

Warren She had new clothes last week ...

Hazel Well, she wanted some more. Isn't she pretty?

Rick She looks like a fairy ...

Stanley Well, I'm sure we'll all get — used to her ... (*He looks at the other two appealingly*) I'm sure we will. In time. I think she looks rather enchanting — as if she was going to a party.

Hazel I'm going to make her a whole wardrobe eventually.

Warren She's shrunk, too. Hasn't she? She's got shorter.

Hazel She was always small. She's the tiniest thing.

Stanley Shall we get on. (*He lays aside the now empty box*) We seem to have lost Novia altogether. Not that it matters since Marcie's not here ...

Hazel I think she fell out somewhere. In the waste disposal.

Stanley (*hastily*) Right. Alric speaks to you all. Since our meeting with Balaac, we have been resting these seven days. We must assume, alas, that Novia, the Newcomer who was with us for so short a time, has been taken by him and may even now be his prisoner. Maybe our task should be to ——

Hazel "gurgles" her drink

— don't do that, Hazel dear ... should be to rescue her ... for God help the child if she should stay for long within the clutches of Balaac. What say we?

Warren 'Tis a good scheme, O Wise One.

Rick Ay.

Stanley Idonia child, what sayest thou?

Hazel (*in a slightly younger voice than before*) Sproing! I think, O Leader, bing-boing, if she be taken by Balaac she is already dead — or worse than dead. Broink! Ding! Idonia foresees this. Better we proceed with our original quest. Sprunk! Forget the silly wench.

Rick (*forcefully*) Nay. No way.

Warren Nay. We canst not do that.

Stanley I agree. Idonia child, you are outnumbered. The will of the majority is that we seek out Balaac and rescue her. You must obey.

Hazel pouts

And so we proceed. Xenon, thou of the Great Sight of the Stranger, what seest thou?

Warren We stand on the edge of the Dead Kingdom of Balaac to the south. Behind us to the north, the Valley of Sighs and the Mountains of Ag. To the east, the Grey River. To the west, the Kingdom of Orrich.

Stanley Tell us, Idonia, Enchantress, Child with the gift of Many Tongues, what seest thou?

Hazel (*sulkily*) Nothing.

Stanley What to the north?

Hazel Nothing.

Stanley What to the south?

Hazel Nothing.

Stanley To the east?

Hazel Nothing.

Stanley Oh, come on, Hazel, for heaven's sake ... To the west?

Hazel Nothing. Dwing! Nothing at all. Dwing! There is no living being in any direction, anywhere. At any time. Dwing! Idonia hath spoken. Now she is silent. Dwing! She is not going on with this quest. She thinks it's a waste of time. Dwing! She is going to take the ice-cream out of the freezer.

Hazel gets up and, without another word, flounces towards the exit, leaving the others still seated, speechless. She flicks on the main lights and exits. Whatever spell there was remaining is broken

Stanley (*switching off the anglepoise*) Well ... maybe she's right. Christmas Eve isn't perhaps the ideal time for ... fighting the forces of ... We will rest, friends. Idonia is right. Maybe by the time of the New Year we will be stronger. Right. Sorry. Shall we — since she's made it — perhaps we ought to go and try some of this orange jelly? Blancmange? I'll bring the sherry. We can take our glasses through ... Perhaps you could both bring a chair — thank you ... After you, please, lead on ...

Stanley ushers Rick and Warren ahead of him. They both go out carrying a chair apiece plus their respective sherry glasses. Stanley follows them with the tray. With a final anxious glance round the room, he switches off the light. In the kitchen, Hazel is singing

The Lights simultaneously come up on Warren's attic. The trap door opens and Warren squeezes through, cautiously. He shuts the trap door quietly. He crosses to his screen and turns up the volume. We hear the single beeping sound. He fades this down. He fades up the speaker. We hear the sound of his mother's gentle snoring. Warren nods. He leaves the speaker faded up. He goes and lies on the bed. He closes his eyes, concentrating deeply

Warren Let it be soon. Let it be soon. Come to me, you beautiful Trilla! Come to me! Marcie! Marcie! Oh, Marcie!

As he lies there ...

Hazel comes back into the darkened sitting-room

Hazel (*seeing the figures still lying on the table*) Tch! Tch! Tch! What are you all doing out of your box? You naughty things. (*She starts to put them away. But scarcely has she started to do so when, in her hands, the creatures appear to develop lives of their own. Thanks to the accompanying dialogue from Hazel — plus a little "incidental" hummed music — the four little people contrive a daring escape off the table-top, down a table-leg and under the table. Their dialogue is barely audible to anyone but Hazel, but if we could hear it, it would probably go something like this:*) Come on, everybody, let's get going ... OK. Here we go, follow me. (*A tiny fanfare*) Over the cliff! Boook! Follow Herwin. Doodle-ee! Here take my hand, Idonia. Come on, Xenon, you slow-coach, don't get left behind. Peep! Help, help. I'm slipping. It's all right, I've got you. Doop! Deep! That's better. (*A dramatic chord*) Nearly there. Wackatow! Look, there's something following us. (*Another chord*) Quick, under the cliff. (*Music*) We'll be safe here. Quang! Wang! he can't see us under here. (*She produces a little more "music" as she and the four little characters vanish under the table. She continues to play quietly*)

Thelma, via the speaker, snorts loudly in her sleep. Warren, who has apparently dozed off as well, wakes with a jolt

Warren (*with a cry*) Marcie! (*He blinks awake*) I saw her! Arnie, I saw her. She was just so beautiful ... (*He enjoys his moment of ecstasy. Something makes him aware of his hands. He holds them up and studies them*) My hands. What's happening to my hands? They're — they're changing. My hands are changing ... I'm starting to change ... (*He rises ecstatically and moves to his console*) I must get it finished. There's very little time. I've got very little time left ... (*He goes to his console and works away feverishly for a moment or two*)

During the next, Warren carefully opens the trap door and descends, closing it behind him

Stanley enters the sitting-room. He sees the game board still out and starts to put it away. There is a tiny fanfare from Hazel under the table. Stanley looks startled. He goes down on his hands and knees and sees Hazel

Stanley Hazel?

Hazel Hallo. Bloon-blip-bloon ...

Stanley What are you doing? What are you doing under there, old love?

Hazel Playing. I'm having a play ... Bloon!

Stanley Having a play?

Hazel With the little people.

Stanley With the little people? Oh, yes. Well, I think it's time for bed now, don't you, old love?

Hazel (*plaintively*) I want to play ...

Stanley Yes, but it's getting rather late, you see. And you've had a long day. Come on. (*He takes her hand and gently draws her out from under the table*) That's it. Tell you what, you take those little people with you, what about that? Would you like to take them up to — to bed with you?

Hazel Yes. Doople-deedle ...

Stanley Good. Come on, then. That's a good girl. We may have to — go out tomorrow, Hazel, to see someone ...

Hazel Where are we going?

Stanley I'll tell you tomorrow. It's a surprise. I'll tell you tomorrow. That's it. Come on, up we go.

During the following, he gently leads Hazel out of the room and upstairs to bed

The Lights cross-fade to Rick's basement. The overhead light is on. The room is empty. There is a knock at the door. There is a brief pause, then another knock. The handle is tested. The door is already unlocked. The door opens and Rick looks inside, slightly cautiously. She enters, carrying a bag, and closes the door behind her. She stands surveying the room, very still, listening

Suddenly we hear footsteps. They are coming from the top of the stairs. Rick waits, tense. Someone comes slowly down the stairs. We see, at length, that it is Marcie. She is holding a suitcase. Her face is red and her eyes swollen from crying

Rick (*softly*) What are you doing?

Marcie (*in a small shaky voice*) I had to borrow a suitcase, I'm sorry.

Rick Where are you going?
Marcie It's — it's probably best ...

We hear further footsteps and Larry appears on the stairs above and behind Marcie

Larry Good-evening. I dropped by to pick up my wife. I hope you've no objections. I thought it was time she got back to a normal healthy relationship. You're just in time to say goodbye. (*He pushes Marcie in front of him*)

Marcie moves forward like a zombie. Rick stands motionless, blocking the doorway. Marcie reaches Rick

Want to say ta-ta, then, do we? I won't look. I'll turn my back. If you'd like to give Marcie one last kiss, Alice.
Rick (*exploding with rage*) You bastard ...
Larry (*laughing*) Now, now ...

His laugh is short-lived. Rick delivers three or four lethal-looking martial-arts blows to Larry's face and body. The whole thing is lightning-fast. Larry goes down like a dead ox. He lies unconscious

Marcie (*in breathless admiration*) Golly!
Rick (*even more amazed*) It works. It actually works.
Marcie How is he?
Rick He's not dead. I don't know why he isn't. Those were all supposed to be lethal blows. I obviously didn't do them quite right ...
Marcie Pretty good ...
Rick Yes, pretty good. Hurt my hand, though ...
Marcie (*concerned*) Is it all right, let me see ... (*She takes Rick's hand*)
Rick It's all right.

Larry starts to come round. He seems to be having trouble breathing through his nose. He makes a snorting noise

Marcie He's waking up. What are we going to do ... ?
Rick It's fine, don't worry.
Marcie But what if he ... what if he ... ?
Rick I'll hit him again, won't I?
Larry (*sitting up and feeling his nose*) You broken my does. You doe dat. You broken by bluddy dose ... You bluddy bitch ... Arrggh! (*He gets up, in some pain. Rick has probably broken his ribs as well. He dabs at his nose with an increasingly bloody handkerchief. To Marcie*) Cub on. Are you cubbing?

Marcie (*looking at them both in turn*) No.

Larry You cub or I'll break your deck, you liddle brick deaser. (*He lurches forward*)

Rick You lay one finger on her and I promise you, you'll never walk again. I'll break both your legs.

Larry hesitates

Come on. Want to try it? Come on.

A moment

Larry (*retreating to the door*) I'll be back — donchoo worry ...

Rick I wouldn't advise it ... Goodbye. Off you go.

Larry opens the outside door and steps out

Larry (*just before he leaves*) You broken by does, you doe. Bluddy desbian dyke bitches ...

Larry goes, closing the door behind him

Marcie (*immediately locking the door*) Are you all right?

Rick (*shrugging nonchalantly*) Yes, yes ...

Marcie You were fantastic.

Rick Well ...

Marcie Do you want anything ... Tea .. or ...

Rick No. I'm OK.(*She sits*)

Marcie (*moving to Rick*) I didn't — I wasn't ... I was only leaving because — because he threatened to hurt you if I didn't. I mean, that was the only reason. I didn't want to go with him.

Rick Whatever. (*She shrugs again*)

Marcie (*smiling*) And I promise you, I never told him about your name. I promise. He saw the note up there. You do believe that, don't you?

Rick Yes. I believe you. Why shouldn't I?

Marcie (*sitting by Rick and taking her hand*)We ought to burn it. Before anyone else reads it. We ought to burn everything up there. Start again. What do you say?

Rick snatches her hand away and rises

Sorry, did I hurt your hand?

Rick No.

Marcie You don't like — people touching you very much, do you?
Rick I don't mind. Why?
Marcie I just wondered.

There is a silence

Rick (*softly*) He used to ... him ... the man my mother lived with ... upstairs ... he used to ... try and touch me. Sometimes. I wasn't that young. I was fourteen. Or fifteen. (*She pauses*)

Marcie waits

Don't tell your mum. Just our secret, Alice. Don't tell your mum. Come on, Alice. There's a good girl. Isn't that nice, Alice? Doesn't that feel good? ... One day he hurt me and I kicked him. And he hit me. And my mum saw the bruise. And she asked me how I got it. So I told her. (*She pauses*) But she didn't believe me. She couldn't believe me, could she? If she believed me, what would that make him? And if he was that, what would that do to her, who couldn't live without him. So he lied — of course — and she believed him. Because that was how she wanted it to be. (*She pauses*) He stayed Mr Wonderful, so what did that make me, eh? A jealous little teenage tart who tried to screw her mother's boyfriend. So she took him away. Away from temptation. Away from me. (*She pauses*) I don't like people touching me very much, no.

Marcie stands looking at Rick. She is very moved, but unsure what to do for the best. Rick looks at her, eventually. She is propped against the table, half sitting, half standing. Marcie smiles weakly. Rick holds out a hand, rather awkwardly. Marcie moves to take it. They stand. Marcie kisses her lightly on the mouth. Rick responds. They smile at each other

Marcie (*suddenly a little awkward, glancing at her watch*) It's Christmas Day, you know. Happy Christmas.
Rick (*pulling away*) Just a second ...
Marcie (*smiling*) Where are you going now?
Rick Wait. (*She rummages in her bag and produces a small parcel, inexpertly wrapped. She holds it out to Marcie rather self-consciously*) Here you are. Happy Christmas.
Marcie Thank you. (*She takes the parcel*) We should wait till the morning really.
Rick Doesn't matter.
Marcie Well, OK. (*She opens the parcel*) What have I got? What have I got? What's this? (*She reveals a small jeweller's box*) Hey! What has she bought me in this lovely little —— (*she breaks off as she sees the contents*) Oh.

Rick (*anxiously*) Is it all right?

Marcie (*a bit stunned*) It's just beautiful. It's lovely. It's gorgeous. (*She takes a small antique pendant out of the box and holds it up*) It's the most beautiful thing I've ever seen. Thank you. Where did you ... ? No, I mustn't ask that.

Rick It was mine. I got given it. By some old aunt. I never wore it.

Marcie But don't you want to keep it?

Rick I don't wear pendants much. I look a bit stupid. Get caught up in the handlebars.

Marcie Well, I'll certainly wear it. (*She kisses Rick*) Thank you. I must try it on ... No, wait, wait a minute. (*She puts the pendant on the table*) You can have just one of yours now. Just one. You can't have the others till tomorrow morning ...

Marcie darts off momentarily, returning with a splendidly wrapped fair-sized parcel

Here you are. I can't even remember what this one is. I certainly haven't got you anything as splendid as that. Here.

Rick Thank you. (*She starts to open the parcel*)

Marcie Read the card. Read the card first.

Rick Oh, yes. (*She does so*) Oh, yes. Thank you.

Marcie I mean it. Every word.

Rick (*slightly embarrassed again*) Thank you. (*She removes the wrapping paper to reveal a cardboard box*)

Marcie (*giggling delightedly*) Oh, I know what this is. It's this. This is for both of us really.

Rick I don't know what this can be. (*She opens the box and takes out a cooking utensil. She stares at it*)

Marcie It's an omelette pan. Do you like it?

Rick (*smiling bravely through her disappointment*) It's great. It's really good.

Marcie It's what we needed, isn't it?

Rick We did. Amazing. (*She waves it vaguely*) Heavy.

Marcie They need to be heavy. It's a good one. Made in France. I'm going to try on my lovely pendant.

Marcie grabs the pendant and hurries off

(*Off*) See what it looks like ...

Rick stands rather crestfallen with her omelette pan, then heads for the exit

(*A delighted cry; off*) Oh, it's gorgeous. It's going to go with practically everything I have.

Rick (*to herself*) Good. (*A look at the pan, ruefully*) So will this.

Rick goes off

The Lights cross-fade to Warren's attic

Warren is emerging through the trap door. He has on dark glasses. He leaves the trap door open and sits at his console. He has an air of a man dealing with an imminent emergency. He presses down his mike switch and speaks, his voice booming down the stairs through numerous speakers

Warren Mother ... Mother ... Are you awake? (*He presses another switch*)

From a loudspeaker on the wall we hear Thelma wake with a start

Thelma (*her voice, startled*) Warren ... what's happening? It's half-past five.
Warren Mother, this is your son Warren speaking. I must ask you for the next few hours not to leave your room unless you are given clearance by me to do so.
Thelma (*her voice*) What are you talking about? It's Christmas morning, Warren ...
Warren I'm sorry, Mother ...
Thelma (*her voice*) I have to cook your dinner ...
Warren There will be no dinner today, Mother. I'm sorry. I am having to switch on the force fields to prevent unauthorized movement around the house ...
Thelma (*her voice*) Warren, I can't stop in here all day. I have to go to Mass.
Warren (*pressing down a switch*) Mother, there is now mains voltage running through your bedroom door handle.
Thelma (*her voice*) Warren, son. Let me try and get Father Kennedy round to see you, would that help ...?
Warren Please remain where you are. I will be monitoring your movements at all times.
Thelma (*her voice*) Warren, please, he'd know what to do for the best, you see. You might need an exorcism ...
Warren That is all, Mother. (*He cuts off both the speaker and the mike. He rises and looks at himself in the mirror. Touching his face*) It's happening. It's happening all over me.

He hurries for the trap door and scrambles off down the ladder

As he does this, the Lights come up on the Inchbridges' sitting-room

Stanley leads Marcie into the room. He has the look of a man who wasn't expecting company. He is in his dressing-gown. He seems a little tireder,

even older than before. Marcie is as spruce and trim as ever. She carries
a bag filled with Christmas parcels. She is wearing her new pendant

Marcie (*entering*) I hope you don't object to people coming round on Christmas morning?

Stanley No, no. It's splendid to see you. It's a lovely surprise ...

Marcie I don't know, at home we just had this tradition ——

Stanley Fine. Please. Sit down.

Marcie Just literally for a second. I've got one or two more people to see. Left Rick fast asleep. She can sleep round the clock if you let her ... Now ... (*she examines her carrier*) Oh, yes. That's Warren's. Called round there just now. I couldn't get a reply. Maybe he and his mother have gone away.

Stanley (*doubtfully*) Possibly.

Marcie (*finding her three gifts*) Here we are. Just little things.

Stanley (*concealing a yawn*) Thank you.

Marcie Didn't wake you up, did I?

Stanley No, no. I've been up for hours. Hazel tends to wake very early these days.

Marcie How is she?

Stanley Oh, fine. Splendid. She's around — somewhere.

Marcie She was looking terrific the last time I saw her ... Look, this is for her. It's just a sort of embroidery kit ... I know she likes sewing and making things ... It might not be her sort of thing at all but ——

Stanley Lovely. It could just be a trifle — complicated — for her ——

Marcie Oh, I shouldn't think so ...

Stanley It has sharp needles and things, does it?

Marcie Oh, yes ...

Stanley Well, we'll see. (*He lays the present aside and turns to another small parcel*) What's this?

Marcie Oh, that's a book for Mr Skate. It's a dictionary. Just a baby one. I know he's fond of words.

Stanley Oh, yes, that's splendid. I'll make sure he gets it.

Marcie Will he be coming home soon?

Stanley Er — probably not for some little while yet. He's a lot better. He's recovered well from the second stroke. He's not yet regained his speech but he's sitting up and taking notice.

Marcie Good. Give him my best wishes.

Stanley I will. (*He picks up the third parcel*)

Marcie That's for you. Now that's really, really, really silly. I just couldn't resist it.

Stanley What on earth is this?

The package reveals a small, inexpensive, unexceptional if quite appealing china or plaster dog

(Literally lost for words) Good heavens!

Marcie Isn't he sweet? I just fell in love with him. I had to buy him for someone and I thought of you. I thought he could be in your game. A talking dog. Have you ever had a talking dog?

Stanley No ...

Marcie You should.

Stanley He's splendid. What a — splendid face. As a matter of fact, I — well, I wasn't expecting to see you today so I haven't even wrapped it properly — just a minute ... *(He rises and goes to the sideboard. He rummages in a drawer, searching for his gift, and finds a small brown paper bag)* Yes, here we are. Not very elegantly wrapped but — here we are, anyway. Forgive the wrapping paper. *(He gives the present to Marcie)*

Marcie takes her present from the bag. It is another pendant. A modern one with nowhere near the value or the style of the one she is wearing

Marcie Oh, you shouldn't have given me this.

Stanley Do you like it?

Marcie It must have been terribly expensive.

Stanley I noticed you wore things like that sometimes.

Marcie Yes, I do. All the time. Look. *(She displays the one she is wearing)*

Stanley Oh, yes. That's really nice. Nicer than that one.

Marcie *(tactfully)* No. They're just — different. Thank you. *(She bends forward to kiss Stanley on the cheek)*

Stanley tries to kiss Marcie on the lips. It is a very clumsy exchange. They both step back in slight embarrassment. As they do this ...

Hazel enters the room. She is crawling on her hands and knees and pushing a toy vehicle of some description

Marcie stares at her in natural surprise. Stanley seems barely to notice her

Hazel *(making car sounds)* ... brrrmmm! Brrrmmm! Brrrmmm! ...

Marcie *(staring in horror at Hazel)* Is she all right? Mrs Inchbridge? Is anything wrong?

Stanley No. She plays like that for hours. *(Loudly)* Hazel! Hazel, darling! *(He indicates the vehicle)* Her Christmas present. Look who's here. Hazel!

Hazel looks up somewhat myopically

Hazel, do you know who this is? It's Marcie. Say hallo. Hallo, Marcie.

Hazel Hallo—mercy ... Bloop! Blooooop!

Marcie Hallo, Mrs ... Hazel. (*Lost for words*) She's — she's ...
Stanley (*picking up the toy dog*) Hazel, what's this? What's this then?
What's this? Do you know what this is?

Hazel extends both her hands to show she wants it

Yes. You tell me what it is first.
Hazel Bow-wow.
Stanley Good. There you are. (*He gives it to her*) What do you say?
Hazel 'kyou.
Stanley Thank you. You play with that. And don't put it in your mouth. (*To
Marcie*) She puts everything in her mouth. She's a terror.
Hazel (*playing*) ... brrrmm. Wooof! Woof! Brrmm!
Stanley Quietly, Hazel. We're trying to talk.

Hazel crawls under the table

That's it. You go under there then.

As Hazel disappears, Stanley reaches down to feel her rather bulky backside

(*To Marcie, apologetically*) Make sure she's dry. She gets a bit damp mid-
mornings.
Hazel (*from under the table*) Beep-beep ..
Marcie Stanley, what's the matter with Hazel exactly? What's happened to
her ...?
Stanley (*impetuously*) Let's talk about us for a minute, could we, please? I
want to talk about us.
Marcie Us?
Stanley Hazel's fine. It's us. You and me. That's what we need to talk about.
Marcie What about?

*At this point, Hazel pushes her vehicle along the ground to Stanley, who even
as he talks, bends and absently pushes it back to her. Promptly Hazel pushes
the vehicle back again, this time to Marcie, who similarly crouches and
pushes it back to Hazel whilst still trying to listen to Stanley. Gradually, whilst
Stanley is still speaking, the three engage in a vehicle exchange, crouching
on the floor and pushing the toy from one to the other. Hazel enjoys this no
end. Marcie tries to concentrate on both at once. Stanley blurts out his
feelings, almost oblivious to what is happening*

Stanley Our — love. My love for you. And — so I hope — your love for
me. I mean — there's no point in trying to pretend otherwise — things have
not been right between Hazel and I — Hazel and me — for years. In fact,
if you want the truth, I don't think they've ever been right. Not since the

day we married. Now, I think I could have put up with it, I think I could, I think I could have seen it through till death us do part. Only one day I meet someone like you — and I'm suddenly offered the chance of escape, the chance to do things I've never had a chance to do before. To give something to someone for a change, something that I know they need from me, would be willing to accept from me. Because unless you meet someone in this life who's prepared to take things from you, how can you decently hope to take things from them in return. And if you're unable to do either of those things, what chance have you ever got of finding happiness? Do you see what I'm saying?

The game stops abruptly. There is silence

Marcie I don't actually know what you're talking about.
Stanley I'm talking about you and me, Marcie. Starting again together somewhere. A new life.
Marcie Living together?
Stanley Yes.
Marcie Me and you?
Stanley Yes.

There is a silence. Hazel bangs the table-leg

Hazel, don't do that, darling. (*To Marcie*) What do you say? Say yes.
Marcie I — I don't know what to say. I had no idea you ... I never thought for a minute you ... I'm — I don't know what to say. It wouldn't work. It's impossible.
Stanley (*stunned*) Impossible? Why? Why?
Marcie Well, we're — just not right, are we ... ? I'm — I mean, I'm — oh, golly, this is difficult to say — I don't want to hurt your feelings but — you're — well, you're old. I mean, much older than me. Aren't you?
Stanley A little. Not that much.
Marcie No, much. Much, much. Really. It wouldn't work — even if — I felt anything — like — which I don't.
Stanley These things have worked before ...
Marcie Oh, yes. But that's only old men wanting a bit of the other before they drop dead, isn't it?
Stanley I'm not like that. I'm not an old man after a bit of the other ...
Marcie I know you're not. That's what I'm saying. You'd want us for life, wouldn't you?
Stanley Of course.
Marcie Well, what about me? By the time I'm at an age where I could really do with someone, someone to look after me, you'd be dead. I mean, that's terribly cruel. But it's true. Isn't it?

Stanley (*crushed*) How old do you think I am? I'm not that old.
Marcie (*kindly*) No, but you will be, Stanley, don't you see? Much sooner than I will.

Silence

I'd better go. (*She rises*)

Stanley remains seated, in a daze

Thank you very, very much for asking me. I'm terribly flattered. (*She picks up her carrier and moves to the door, leaving her locket on the table, the chain dangling over the edge. She stoops to look under the table*) Goodbye, Hazel. Happy Christmas.
Hazel Happy Mistmas — Hismas — Kissmas ...
Marcie (*just as she is going*) Stanley — you are going to — let someone — have a look at Hazel, aren't you? Examine her. I mean, she needs help, doesn't she? There's something very wrong. Don't you think so?
Stanley (*wearily*) God knows. I don't know. All I know is she's happy, Marcie. She's happier than she's ever been in her whole life. Can that be wrong?
Marcie Well. Yes. I still think she should see someone. I really do. Still, it's up to you. She's your wife. Bye.
Stanley (*sadly*) Bye.

Marcie goes

Hazel sings and chortles and mutters under the table. Stanley rises to the window to watch Marcie leave. As he stands there, Hazel's little fist comes from under the table. She grabs the end of the locket chain and pulls it off. The sound causes Stanley to turn

Hazel, what are you doing? What have you got now?

Hazel puts the locket in her mouth

Hazel, take that out of your mouth at once. Come on. Come on. Or else I'll get cross. (*He bends under the table and prises the locket from Hazel's jaws*) That's it. That's better, thank you. Not lockets. Mustn't eat lockets. Not for mouths ... Aaarrgg! (*He straightens up and his back gives*) Oh, oh. That's agony. Come on, Hazel, in the kitchen. Ow! Ow! Ow! Come on. (*He is in some pain*)

Hazel comes out from under the table. She holds up her arms to be carried

No, darling, I can't carry you. You're much too heavy, you see? Why do you think my back's hurting? You'll have to crawl, come on. I'll give you a biscuit. Come on, in the kitchen. (*He moves to the doorway and stops*)

Hazel crawls ahead of Stanley. As she passes, he pushes her bottom to encourage her on her way

(*Irritably, wiping his hand on his dressing-gown*) Oh, Hazel, don't tell me you need changing as well ...

Hazel crawls off, Stanley limping behind her

Warren appears, crawling up the ladder. He is breathing heavily — he appears to be running some sort of fever. He presses the mike and speaker switches

Warren (*with difficulty*) Mother, hold on. It won't be for much longer, I promise you.
Thelma (*her voice coming from the speaker*) I'm praying for you, son. I'm praying for you. Would you like a nice hot cup of tea?
Warren Please, Mother. Later, later. I'm tired. I'm going to have to save my strength. (*He switches off the speaker and the mike. He half crawls to the bed. He leans against it, huddled on the floor, shivering, half in a sort of feverish trance*)

The Lights come up in the basement. It is daytime

Rick comes downstairs from the house. She is in her work clothes and very dirty and tired. She is lugging two huge plastic sacks of rubbish. She drags them to the back door

Marcie (*calling from upstairs*) Darling!
Rick (*yelling*) Hallo!
Marcie When you come up can you bring the vacuum cleaner?
Rick (*yelling*) OK.

During the following, she lugs the sacks out into the area outside

(*To herself*) Oh, my God. What have we started?

She exits

Marcie appears on the stairs. She has on her headscarf and heavy-duty rubber gloves

Marcie Darling! Rick!

Rick reappears

Rick Yeah.
Marcie You managing all right?
Rick Yes, I'm OK.
Marcie Don't overtire yourself, darling. Rest if you need to.
Rick (*plodding towards the kitchen*) I will.
Marcie Bad news. I'm afraid there's three more bags up here.

Rick goes off

Rick (*as she goes*) Yes, OK.
Marcie There's mountains to get rid of. We may need to get a skip
eventually, if they won't take it away.

Marcie goes off upstairs

Rick reappears with the (new) vacuum cleaner. She heads for the stairs

(*Off, upstairs*) Rick! Rick, darling.
Rick Hallo.
Marcie (*off*) Do you feel strong enough to move the sideboard now, please?
Rick Yes, yes, yes ...
Marcie (*off*) Sorry, darling ...

Rick limps off wearily

*The Lights fade on the basement. In the attic, the computer suddenly sets off
several alarms at once. Warren comes out of his daze. He leaps up and kills
the alarms. As he does so he becomes aware of his "new" self*

Warren (*incredulously*) It's happened. It's worked. It's worked. (*He looks
in the mirror*) My God, look at me. Look at me. (*He laughs with joy*) I'm
a Lak! I'm a Lak! I'm a full-grown Lak! Marcie! Look at me now, Marcie!
(*He remembers*) Mother ... Mother!

*He goes to the console and presses both the mike and the speaker switches.
There is a low indistinct moaning from the speaker: the sound of Thelma
recovering*

Mother! Mother!

Thelma (*weakly, from the speaker*) Warren? Is that you?

Warren Are you all right ...?

Thelma (*from the speaker*) I tried to open the door. I was thrown across the room ...

Warren Mother, I told you to stay where you were ...

Thelma (*from the speaker*) I needed the toilet, Warren. I've been waiting for ages. Are you all right, son? How are you? I thought you'd died.

Warren I'm fine, Mother. Happy Christmas. And God bless us every one.

Thelma (*from the speaker*) Warren, it's Boxing Day.

Warren Is it? (*startled*) Is it? (*He starts to switch things off*) Mother, I'm switching everything off now. You can come out.

Thelma (*from the speaker*) Oh, thank heavens ...

Warren Mother ...

Thelma (*from the speaker*) Yes.

Warren Make us both a cup of tea.

Thelma (*radiantly, from the speaker*) Oh, I will. I will, son. As soon as I've ... I'll bring it up to you.

Warren No, you won't. I'll come down and have it with you. We'll have tea together, Mother. What about that?

Thelma (*ecstatically, from the speaker*) Oh, dear God! It's a miracle.

Warren switches off the mike and the speaker. He laughs excitedly. He has another look in the mirror at himself

Warren (*joyously*) Marcie ... Look at me now, Marcie. Can you see me? It's the real me! (*His laughter slowly dies. A thought has occurred. In growing alarm*) What if she can't see me? What if she can't see me ...?

With this sobering thought he starts to descend the ladder

In the Inchbridges' sitting-room it is now evening. The lights are on

Rick carries through the two kitchen chairs. Her image has altered somewhat — presumably Marcie's influence. Instead of the anonymous, classless uniform, she is now off-the-peg slightly trendy. No danger of a dress but a sharp, slightly "macho" outfit, perhaps in leather

Stanley follows her in with the anglepoise. He has a walking-stick and appears to be moving with some difficulty. He's still in his dressing-gown. He seems older and greyer altogether

Stanley (*as they enter*) Thanks so much ... I'm sorry I'm absolutely useless at the moment ...

Rick Can you manage?

Stanley Yes, it's this — bloody back — pardon the language. It's a trapped nerve, they think. Which makes it impossible to do practically anything. Can't even dress myself ...

Rick (*taking the anglepoise*) I'll do that. (*She plugs the light in and switches it on*)

Stanley Thank you. (*He sits*) You're looking good, if you don't mind my saying so.

Rick (*unused to compliments*) Oh, yes.

Stanley Nice hair. And — er, the ... (*he indicates her outfit*)

Rick Oh. Yes. I got it in the sale. Marcie persuaded me to buy it.

Stanley (*dully*) How is Marcie?

Rick (*evasively*) Fine, she's fine.

Stanley Good.

Rick She said she might look in later.

Stanley Ah. Good.

During the following, Rick gets out the board and the four figures

Warren enters carrying Hazel. She is curled up like a baby. She is very sleepy and looks fresh from her bath. Her hair is soft and fluffy, her face pink and contented. Warren is barely recognizable. He has on thick green gauntlets and a green ski mask. No portion of him is actually visible

It will be noticeable — if it wasn't already — that the four now resemble their playing images quite closely

Warren My, you're a heavy girl, aren't you?

Hazel (*singing happily*) Doo-boo-boo-boo ...

Stanley Thank you, Warren. She doesn't need to be carried, she can walk perfectly well. Can't you, you naughty girl ...? Put her in the chair there, Warren, put her in the chair. She can sit up on her own, she's a big girl.

Warren sits Hazel in the chair. He is very good with Hazel

Warren She is. There you are. You sit there. What do you say?

Hazel 'kyou.

Warren Thank you, that's right. Well done. Don't suck your thumb or it'll fall off, won't it? Shall I do the lights, Mr Inchbridge?

Stanley Would you, Warren? Thank you.

Warren switches off the overhead lights. They gather round the table

It's just a skin condition you've got, is it, Warren?

Warren Yes, that sort of thing, Mr Inchbridge.

Stanley Are you seeing someone about it?

Warren Well, apparently, it'll just be a matter of time. I have to keep it covered up, though.

Rick Permanently?

Warren Yes. At present.

Stanley Awkward.

Warren I get a few looks from people.

Stanley You would. All right, we'd better get it over with, I suppose. This is a sad occasion, really — after all these years, but ——

Hazel starts banging the table

Don't do that, Hazel ... Warren, give her Idonia to play with, would you?

Warren (*doing so*) There you are.

Hazel (*delighted*) Idonia ...

Warren Yes, you play with that.

Hazel Idonia ...

Stanley Friends, we all know why we're here. The Game — this Game that's given us so much pleasure and excitement for — five years? — more than that — hath — has finally run its course. As I think was clearly demonstrated when we last met — the board is now empty for us — Balaac is finally dead. Our quest is over and Idonia, Xenon, Herwin, Alric must go back in their box for ever ...

Hazel bangs again

Hazel, don't do that or I'll have to put you to bed.

Warren I'll take her, Mr Inchbridge, I'll take her ...

Stanley Thank you, Warren, that's very kind.

Warren takes Hazel on to his knees. She croons softly

There, Hazel, aren't you lucky? You're a spoilt girl, aren't you? So are we agreed, friends, the Game is concluded?

Rick (*sadly*) Agreed.

Warren (*gloomily*) Agreed. (*Gently*) You agree, don't you, Hazel?

Hazel (*in a tiny sleepy voice*) Yeth.

Warren She agreed.

Stanley Well, that's it. I thought perhaps we might all take our own figures away with us. As a memento. Would that be a nice idea? Yes.

They all pick up their pieces. Hazel still clutches hers

So.

None of them feels like moving. They all sit and stare at the board rather sadly

Suddenly Marcie enters and switches on the overhead lights. They all jump

Marcie Hey, sorry — it's only me. It was so quiet in here I thought you'd all ... The door was open. You all OK?
Stanley Yes.
Rick Yes.
Warren Fine.
Marcie Who's that? Is that Warren?
Warren Yes.
Marcie Why are you like that?
Stanley He has a skin condition.
Marcie What sort of skin condition?
Warren One all over my skin ...
Marcie Let's have a look ...
Warren No, no, it's OK.
Rick (*feebly*) Leave him ...
Marcie Have you been to see anyone about it?
Warren No, no, honestly ... it's ...
Marcie Well, you should. (*Firmly*) Warren! Let me have a look. Come on! Let me see, at once! Put her down. And take that thing off.

Warren puts Hazel back in her chair

Come on! Come into the light.

Warren moves to her. Marcie waits. Slowly he takes off his gloves, then his mask. His face, of course, is perfectly normal. Marcie tilts his face and examines it sternly and critically like a fierce nurse

Warren (*anxiously*) Can you see anything?
Marcie Nothing. You look just the same as usual to me. You stupid thing. It's all in your head. (*To Rick*) Darling, I'm leaving the shopping with you, all right? Can you bring it home on the bike?
Rick Yes.
Marcie Don't be too late, will you?
Rick No.
Marcie 'night, all. 'night, Stanley. Night-night, Hazel.

Hazel blows a raspberry

Oh, that's not a very nice thing to do, Hazel, is it? Naughty girl. I'll switch this out again, shall I? 'night.

Marcie switches off the overhead lights and goes

There is a silence. Hazel has still been clutching Idonia in her hand. She clumps it down suddenly on the board. The other three stare. Then, as if by silent agreement, in turn, Rick replaces Herwin on the board; Warren replaces Xenon; Stanley finally replaces Alric

Stanley (*softly*) Onwards?
Warren Onwards.
Rick Onwards.
Hazel (*with a childish giggle*) Onwards!

Black-out

FURNITURE AND PROPERTY LIST

ACT I
Scene i

On stage: THE INCHBRIDGES' SITTING-ROOM
Two- or three-piece suite
One or two occasional tables
Four upright chairs
Drop-leaf table. *On it*: game board, four model figures (see p.1), box. *Clipped to table*: anglepoise lamp (practical)
Coal-effect gas or electric fire
Chandelier (practical)
One or two table or standard lamps (practical)
Sideboard. *On it*: foolscap envelope containing Warren's manuscript. *In sideboard*: table mats, cruet

RICK'S BASEMENT
Camp bed with duvet
Small table
Easy chair
Upright chair
Small electric fire
Junk
Tin opener
Carrier bag. *In it*: tin of soup or vegetables
Spoon

WARREN'S ATTIC
Computers and computer-driven machinery
Swivel chair
Small bed
Computer magazines and books

Off stage: THE INCHBRIDGES' SITTING-ROOM
Tray. *On it*: sandwiches wrapped in cling-film, mug of milk covered in clingfilm (**Hazel**)

WARREN'S ATTIC
Doorstep sandwich (**Warren**)
Mug of cocoa (**Thelma**)

SCENE 2

Set: THE INCHBRIDGES' SITTING-ROOM
              Newspaper for Austen
              Foolscap envelope. *In it*: **Warren**'s manuscript

Off stage: Fistful of cutlery (**Hazel**)
              Anglepoise lamp (**Stanley**)
              Motor cycle helmets (**Rick** and **Marcie**)
              Plate of sandwiches (**Hazel**)
              "New-look" Idonia figure (**Hazel**)
              Small game figure (**Marcie**)

Personal: **Warren**: computer print-out sheets
              Larry: key

ACT II

Set: THE INCHBRIDGES' SITTING-ROOM
              Newspaper for **Austen**
              New Idonia figure in game box
              Pendant in paper bag in sideboard

Off stage   THE INCHBRIDGES' SITTING-ROOM
              Small package (**Stanley**)
              Jam-jar of dandelions (**Hazel**)
              Workbasket (**Hazel**)
              Doll's dress (**Hazel**)
              Tray. *On it*: bottle of sherry, four glasses (**Stanley**)
              Anglepoise lamp (**Warren**)
              Tall glass of fruit squash with straw (**Hazel**)
              Bag full of Christmas presents including a small plaster dog
                (**Marcie**)
              Toy vehicle (**Hazel**)

              RICK'S BASEMENT
              Two bowls (**Rick**)
              Two spoons (**Rick**)
              Salt and pepper mills (**Rick**)

Saucepan of soup (**Rick**)
Eight large carrier bags (**Marcie**)
Two large square parcels (**Marcie**)
Two mugs of coffee (**Rick**)
Suitcase (**Marcie**)
Bag. *In it*: inexpertly wrapped pendant in jeweller's box (**Rick**)
Splendidly wrapped, boxed omelette pan with card attached
  (**Marcie**)
Two huge plastic sacks of rubbish (**Rick**)
Vacuum cleaner (**Rick**)

WARREN'S ATTIC
Various items of wiring, including cable on drum (**Warren**)
Wiring diagram (**Warren**)

Personal: **Larry**: blood capsule, handkerchief
        Marcie: wrist-watch
        Warren: dark glasses

LIGHTING PLOT

Practical fittings required: THE INCHBRIDGES' SITTING-ROOM: chandelier, one
or two table or standard lamps, clip-on anglepoise lamp
RICK'S BASEMENT: overhead naked bulb
WARREN'S ATTIC: computer screens

Three rooms. Exterior backing to the Inchbridges' sitting-room and RICK's
basement

ACT I, SCENE 1

To open: Anglepoise lamp on table only

Cue 1	**Hazel** switches on the overhead lights *Snap on overhead lights in sitting-room*	(Page 4)
Cue 2	**Stanley** unplugs anglepoise lamp *Snap off anglepoise lamp*	(Page 4)
Cue 3	**Austen**: "Don't mind me." *Fade lights slightly on* **Austen**	(Page 10)
Cue 4	**Rick** switches on light in basement *Snap on light in basement; occasional effect* *of passing traffic throughout scene*	(Page 11)
Cue 5	**Rick** resumes her meal *Fade lights slightly on* **Rick**; *bring up computer* *glow in* **Warren**'*s attic, then general lighting*	(Page 11)
Cue 6	**Warren** starts to type furiously *Cross-fade to* **Rick**'*s basement with passing* *traffic effect*	(Page 12)
Cue 7	Distant door-slam; silence *Cross-fade to* **Inchbridges'** *sitting-room*	(Page 12)
Cue 8	**Hazel** switches off overhead lights *Cross-fade to* **Warren**'*s attic*	(Page 13)
Cue 9	**Warren** lies back *Bring up dim lights on* **Inchbridges'** *sitting-room* *with street-lamp effect from outside*	(Page 14)

| *Cue* 10 | **Hazel** looks out of the window
Bring up lights on basement | (Page 14) |

| *Cue* 11 | **Ken's voice**: "Alice! Alice! Alice!"; pause
Fade lights on basement and attic | (Page 14) |

| *Cue* 12 | **Hazel** and **Stanley** stand close together
Bring up lights on basement and attic | (Page 15) |

| *Cue* 13 | **Rick**: "I'll turn out the light." She does so
Snap off basement lights except exterior backing | (Page 23) |

| *Cue* 14 | **Rick** curls up at the end of the bed
Fade lights on all areas | (Page 25) |

ACT I, Scene 2

To open: General interior lighting in Inchbridges' sitting-room only

| *Cue* 15 | **Stanley** switches on the anglepoise lamp
Snap on anglepoise lamp | (Page 26) |

| *Cue* 16 | **Stanley** switches off overhead lights
Snap off overhead lights in sitting-room | (Page 31) |

| *Cue* 17 | **Austen** switches on overhead lights
Snap on overhead lights in sitting-room | (Page 34) |

| *Cue* 18 | Anglepoise is switched off
Snap off anglepoise lamp | (Page 34) |

| *Cue* 19 | **Marcie** and **Stanley** go out
*Bring up outside street lights and dim interior
   lighting on **Rick**'s basement* | (Page 38) |

| *Cue* 20 | **Rick** lies on the bed
*Bring up lights on **Warren**'s attic* | (Page 39) |

| *Cue* 21 | **Rick** turns on the light
Snap on basement lights | (Page 40) |

| *Cue* 22 | **Austen** leaves the room
*Dim lights in the **Inchbridges'** sitting-room* | (Page 42) |

Cue 23   **Larry** switches off the light   (Page 45)
            Snap off overhead lights in basement; dim light remains

Cue 24   **Warren** bolts the trap door   (Page 46)
            Fade lights on attic

Cue 25   **Rick**: "I'll kill the bastard."   (Page 48)
            *Swift cross-fade from **Rick**'s basement to*
            the Inchbridges' sitting-room

Cue 26   **Marcie** switches off the overhead lights   (Page 48)
            Snap off the overhead lights

Cue 27   **Marcie**: "Fantastic."   (Page 51)
            Black-out

ACT II

To open: General lighting on all areas

Cue 28   **Warren** switches on computer screen   (Page 56)
            Bring up computer glow effect

Cue 29   **Marcie** and **Rick** climb the stairs together   (Page 68)
            Fade lights on attic and basement

Cue 30   **Warren** switches on anglepoise lamp   (Page 68)
            Snap on anglepoise lamp

Cue 31   **Warren** switches off overhead lights   (Page 70)
            Snap off overhead lights

Cue 32   **Hazel** switches on overhead lights   (Page 72)
            Snap on overhead lights

Cue 33   **Stanley** switches off anglepoise lamp   (Page 72)
            Snap off anglepoise lamp

Cue 34   **Stanley** switches off overhead lights   (Page 72)
            Snap off sitting-room overhead lights;
            *bring up lights on **Warren**'s attic*

Cue 35	**Stanley** leads **Hazel** off	(Page 74)
	Cross-fade to **Rick**'s *basement*	
Cue 36	**Rick** exits	(Page 79)
	Cross-fade to **Warren**'s *attic*	
Cue 37	**Warren** scrambles down the ladder	(Page 79)
	The lights come up on the **Inchbridges'** *sitting-room*	
Cue 38	**Warren** leans against the bed	(Page 85)
	The lights come up on **Rick**'s *basement*	
Cue 39	**Rick** limps off wearily	(Page 86)
	Fade lights on basement	
Cue 40	**Warren** descends the ladder	(Page 87)
	Change sitting-room lights to evening effect	
Cue 41	**Rick** switches on the anglepoise	(Page 88)
	Snap on anglepoise	
Cue 42	**Warren** switches off the overhead lights	(Page 88)
	Snap off overhead lights	
Cue 43	**Marcie** switches on overhead lights	(Page 90)
	Snap on overhead light	
Cue 44	**Marcie** switches off overhead lights	(Page 91)
	Snap off overhead lights	
Cue 45	**Hazel**: "Onwards!"	(Page 91)
	Black-out	

EFFECTS PLOT

ACT I

Cue 1   **Rick** lets herself into basement area   (Page 11)
Dripping of distant tap; occasional traffic passing above

Cue 2   **Rick** eats from the tin   (Page 11)
Woman's footsteps scurry overhead

Cue 3   Lights fade on **Rick**'s basement   (Page 11)
Fade tap and traffic noises

Cue 4   Lights cross-fade to **Rick**'s basement   (Page 12)
Resume tap and traffic noises; then footsteps, door slams and dialogue as p. 12

Cue 5   Lights cross-fade to **Inchbridges'** sitting-room (Page 12)
Distant sound of water tank refilling

Cue 6   **Rick** climbs into bed   (Page 14)
Man's footsteps and dialogue as p.14

Cue 7   **Stanley** clamps the anglepoise to the table   (Page 26)
Doorbell

Cue 8   **Warren**: "For menial duties."   (Page 27)
Doorbell

Cue 9   **Warren**: "I cannot yet see him."   (Page 50)
Faint sound of wind, building to a crescendo during dialogue p.50

Cue 10   **Rick**: "I'm ready ... Let him come ... "   (Page 50)
Fade in growing thunderous roar, building to a wail

Cue 11   **Hazel** screams   (Page 51)
Final thunderous explosion

ACT II

Cue 12	**Warren** switches on screen *Beeping sound*	(Page 56)
Cue 13	**Stanley**: "What have I done?" *Doorbell*	(Page 59)
Cue 14	**Warren** turns up computer screen volume *Beeping sound, becoming more rapid*	(Page 60)
Cue 15	**Warren** turns down volume *Decrease volume of beeping sound*	(Page 60)
Cue 16	**Warren** turns up the volume *Double beeps*	(Page 60)
Cue 17	**Warren** turns down the screen volume *Fade double beeps*	(Page 60)
Cue 18	**Warren** goes back to his screen *Double beeps as before*	(Page 63)
Cue 19	**Warren** presses down microphone switch *Amplify **Warren**'s speech p. 66*	(Page 66)
Cue 20	Lights concentrate on **Inchbridges'** sitting-room *Christmas carol recording*	(Page 68)
Cue 21	**Rick**: "Yes." Pause *Carol recording stops*	(Page 70)
Cue 22	**Warren** turns up screen volume, then fades it *Single beeping sound, fading when ready*	(Page 73)
Cue 23	**Warren** fades up speaker *Sound of **Thelma**'s gentle snoring, continuing under following*	(Page 73)
Cue 24	**Hazel** vanishes under the table *Sound of **Thelma** snoring loudly in her sleep*	(Page 73)

Cue 25	**Warren** presses down microphone switch	(Page 79)
	Warren's *dialogue amplified,* **Thelma**'s *voice over speakers as p. 79*	
Cue 26	**Warren** presses mike and speaker switches	(Page 85)
	Warren's *dialogue amplified,* **Thelma**'s *voice over speakers as p. 85*	
Cue 27	Lights fade on basement	(Page 86)
	Alarms go off in **Warren**'s *attic*	
Cue 28	**Warren** kills the alarms	(Page 86)
	Snap off alarms	
Cue 29	**Warren** presses mike and speaker switches	(Page 86)
	Warren's *dialogue amplified,* **Thelma**'s *voice over speakers as p. 86-87*	